THE CCESS

Tom Hopki... ...ching sales
training skil... ...rld's leading general s... ...ons of sales
and sales management professionals succeed beyond
their wildest dreams. Over two million people on four
continents have attended his high energy live seminars.
His audio and video programmes are used by professionals and major corporations all over the world. His
first book, *How to Master the Art of Selling*, has sold
over a million copies and is considered by many to be
required reading for anyone in sales.

TOM HOPKINS

The Official
Guide to Success

Edited by Warren Jamison

HarperCollins*Publishers*

HarperCollins*Publishers*
77–85 Fulham Palace Road,
Hammersmith, London W6 8JB

This paperback edition 1994
3 5 7 9 8 6 4 2

Previously published in paperback by Grafton 1985
Reprinted eight times

This edition published by arrangement with
Warner Books Inc., New York

Copyright © Champion Press 1982

The Author asserts the moral right to
be identified as the author of this work

ISBN 0 586 06315 3

Set in Times

Printed in Great Britain by
HarperCollinsManufacturing Glasgow

*Inside your skin is a far more interesting,
energetic and successful person than
you now believe yourself to be.
This book is dedicated to
that you.*

Contents

x   *Contents*

Introduction

A few years ago, in Kansas City for a speaking engagement, I was passing through the hotel lobby when I heard sounds of enthusiastic applause coming from a ballroom.

I asked the man at the door who was speaking to the large crowd, and his reply was 'Tom Hopkins, and he is the greatest.' I was unable to resist the impulse to slip into a seat, and had great trouble finding one.

I listened with admiration to Tom as he handled a motivational meeting masterfully. It was highly inspirational, very practical and, of course, positive in nature.

I had heard of Tom Hopkins for several years, and subsequent to this incident have followed his career with admiration. I think he is one of the best motivational speakers on the American platform today.

Throughout my own life I have tried to persuade people of the great potential that has been built into them by their Creator. And I have tried to outline techniques of faith and thinking that would help release such potential.

Some years ago I wrote a book called 'The Power of Positive Thinking' which contained my own philosophy of successful living. I am flattered that Tom Hopkins says he read this book and others in his early years and that he has been helped by them in his personal and business life.

It has encouraged me that this brilliant young speaker and writer persuades his readers and listeners to employ the principles of positive thinking in their own lives.

I am delighted that Tom Hopkins has written a new book, 'The Official Guide to Success, Volume One.' In this volume he shows effectively how the time-tested principles of success in which he and I believe may be geared to the complex demands of our contemporary generation.

Mr Tom Hopkins has the ability to relate the long proven concepts and ideas for gaining happiness and success, so that his generation can understand and use these basic principles creatively.

In these pages he has outlined a workable guide to success, and in my judgment anyone seeking fulfilment in their lives will find practical and valuable help in the study of Tom Hopkins' 'The Official Guide to Success, Volume One.' I know that as this book goes out among people everywhere, it will change the lives of many for the better.

NORMAN VINCENT PEALE

1 How to flip your switch from *lose* to *win*

Throughout our entire lives, we operate under a set of instructions. Everything we choose to do is governed by them. So is almost everything that happens to us, and almost everything we think we're forced to do.

Since the instructions other people give us after childhood have no effect on our personalities beyond the impact we give those instructions by repeating them inside our own heads, all our self-instructions fall into only three categories:

(1) Instincts.
(2) Whatever someone else pounded into us during our childhood.
(3) Everything we've pounded into our own personalities since childhood.

That makes our self-instructions sound simple. They're not. Our self-instructions are extremely complex. The most advanced researchers in this field claim no more than a general understanding of their processes and interconnections.

But one fact *is* simple. Where our self-instructions are negative, our achievements will be negative. That is, we will lose in our negative instruction areas because we can succeed there only by failing. In other words, we will do what we have programmed ourselves to do.

On the other hand, where our self-instructions are positive we will achieve much. We'll win far more often than we'll lose. We'll do that because we've programmed ourselves to achieve and to win in that area of our activities.

Would you like to change your self-instructions in the areas where you're now losing?

Fortunately, we don't have to wait for science to gain a complete understanding of these instructions before we can get started on changing them. If we're perfectly satisfied in every way with ourselves, our lives, and our achievements, we won't want to change our instructions. Few people who feel that way will open this book. Most of us want to see a great amount of improvement in our lives and our achievements, and we want to see that improvement fast. We're even willing to think about changing ourselves a bit if it'll help bring those improvements about, aren't we?

The changes start with our goals. Nobody is without goals. The unfortunate alcoholic who slept on a park bench last night owns a goal: to acquire another jug of wine. The temporarily-broke tycoon who has made and lost a dozen fortunes owns a goal: to acquire another fortune. They'll both reach their goals. Why? Because their self-instructions not only allow them to, they require them to.

To get an understanding of how we can change our instructions to ourselves, let's look at how they keep us moving down the road we've chosen to travel – again, by heeding those self-instructions. The method is so simple, and we all use it so constantly all our lives, that we tend to forget it.

Our self-instructions control us because we keep repeating them over and over to ourselves – and often to anyone else we can get to listen. Hour after hour, that little voice in our head keeps telling us things:

'I better not try that.'
'They'd probably just turn me down anyway.'
'I've got to do this or I'm a goner.'
'She wouldn't go out with me.'
'What if I call him and he says no?'
'I don't have a chance to win this one now.'
'If I miss the next one, I've had it.'

I could list thousands of these tension-building and confidence-destroying instructions that many of us wash through our brains all day every day. No wonder we're afraid to try new things – we always lose when we do. Which is what we expected. Which is why we did. It's a closed loop. Expected failure keeps on breeding more failure, which in turn breeds more expectations of failure.

We can just as well tell ourselves to succeed.

That is, we can just as well set ourselves up to keep on breeding the expectation of success, which will breed success, which will breed more expectation of success. That's a closed loop too, and it's what flipping our switch from lose to win is all about.

We start by telling ourselves that we can do it. The basic concept is that simple, although the technique for doing it successfully is a bit more complicated. We'll get into that in a moment. If you'll follow the system thoroughly enough, that is, often enough and with enough emotional force, it really will flip your switch from lose to win. The fantastic part is that – once you have yourself organized to do it, you'll spend less than five minutes a day on it.

It won't work if you decide to make sure it won't work. Unfortunately, unless this system is helping you, it's hurting you. Why? Because there's no way you can shut that little voice inside your head off. As long as you're conscious, it'll keep on telling you to succeed or fail, to stay healthy or get sick, to take a carefully-prepared-for risk or to let it all ride on a wild gamble. That voice is always there, telling you to lose or win.

So let's get on with winning more often. Here's how to make the good things start happening sooner.

Make up a set of new self-instructions. However, this set will be vastly different from all the instructions you've been giving yourself throughout your life up to now. The difference is that these instructions will be carefully thought through. Then they'll be written out. Finally, and most importantly, they'll be reviewed frequently as a conscious act. In other words, they are different because they are completely under your control. This means that you can make them completely positive to what you want to do now.

Write your new self-instructions on 3 × 5 inch cards, one to a card. Write things like:

'Today I'll meet the right people in the right place at the right time for the betterment of all.'

'People like me. It's amazing, but nearly everyone I meet really likes me right off. Of course, I like almost everyone I meet right away too. I guess the way I feel about people shows.'

'I always prepare thoroughly for every important thing that I do. This is one reason why I – ' (Finish this one to fit your own unique situation.) ' – win so many of my cases.' ' – close so many sales.' ' – accomplish so much in my business.'

'I always leave early for an appointment so I'll have time to psyche myself up before I get there.'

'I always do the thing I least want to do first, so it doesn't hang over me and spoil my whole day.'

'Every day, I get closer to my goals.'

The more specific your new self-instructions are, the more they'll help you change what you want to change. 'I get up feeling great every morning at six A.M.' 'I make ten calls a day.' 'I run a mile every day.'

There are some rules you must follow to make this system work for you:

1. Don't worry about the truth of your self-instructions. Keep in mind that they are about who you want to be, not who you are today.

2. Cast your self-instructions in the here and now: 'I run a mile every day.' If you put your instruction in the future, it won't take effect. 'Pretty soon I'm going to start running a mile every day,' doesn't work because *pretty soon* never comes.

3. Keep your self-instructions free of guilt and pressure: Use 'I get up feeling great every morning at six' instead of 'I've got to get up at six no matter what.'

4. Pack them with emotion: 'I don't eat those yukky, gooey pastries.'

5. Concentrate on at least ten, but no more than twenty, self-instructions at a time. When you're satisfied that one of them is now a firm part of your highly successful new nature, drop its card from the pack. Then put a new one in its place.

6. Build your confidence in this system by starting with several easy ones. Little things that drive your spouse crazy, like not putting the cap back on the toothpaste, are terrific for proving to

yourself that the system really works. Always keep a few easy ones in the pile so you won't overwhelm yourself.

7. Emphasize confidence in your new self-instructions: 'I always make a fine impression because I know my stuff, I dress professionally, and I'm sensitive to people.'

8. Relaxation and alertness are the keys to superior performance. Emphasize them in your new self-instructions: 'I do everything with smooth, relaxed alertness.'

9. Look through your own eyes as you see yourself performing with calm confidence.

10. Aim for the mark, not beyond it. If you're overweight and want to lose a few bulges, don't keep telling yourself that you never eat and you're just skin and bones – you're likely to starve yourself to death. Pick the weight you want. Then choose a sensible rate of weight loss, and start seeing yourself enjoying life at the weight you want to be. If you make your vision of the rewards of losing weight vivid enough, you'll avoid that extra helping and all those other avoidable calories, and you'll get down to your chosen weight right on schedule. It's all a matter of what you instruct yourself to really want. With all self-instructions relating to health and diet, be sure to consult your doctor before you make any changes.

11. Carry your pack of self-instruction cards with you. Review them as soon as you can in the morning, whenever you have a spare moment during the day, and before you go to bed at night.

This works. Beautifully. Constantly. With astonishing power. It does all this because it allows you to guide your mind the way your mind functions. But you have to use this system to get its benefits – you have to review your new self-instructions at least three times a day. And you have to take enough time to visualize being who and what that instruction is about with keen emotional force. After a few days' practice, it will only take two or three seconds for each one.

And you have to want to make this system work for you. Do you?

2   The golden dozen – this easy system will send you straight up

Here's the best way I've ever found to pull the best performance out of yourself. It's an extremely simple method. Not easy, simple. First, hang copies of these twelve words where you'll see them at work, in your car, and at your home base:

I MUST DO THE MOST PRODUCTIVE THING POSSIBLE AT EVERY GIVEN MOMENT.

Now comes the important part:

Dedicate yourself to living that declaration.

It doesn't change anything to look at those words once in a while and think. 'That's what I'm going to start doing just as soon as I can get myself together.' If you really want to achieve, start living by that dozen words *now*.

Doing so requires only four steps. Imagine – only four steps to all the success you want – nothing could be more simple, could it? But let's get one thing clear at this point: Doing the most productive thing possible means just that – the *most productive* thing. Not make work. Not look busy. Not get by. Not put off. But doing the most productive thing *possible* at that given moment, no matter how distasteful, hard or worrisome the thing might be. This often means tying into a knotty problem, facing up to an unpleasant task, or heading into a likely rejection. It means shooting for the top when you know you should but are afraid to. It means preparing when you need to prepare and doing when you need to do. That's why I say it isn't easy, and why so few people follow it. It is simple, though. Anyone can do it – you just have to want to. Here's how. Consciously repeat these four steps minute by minute until they become second nature:

(1) Tell yourself, 'I must do the most productive thing possible at every given moment.'
(2) Decide what the most productive thing is.
(3) Do it.
(4) When you've pushed that thing as far forward as you can right now, go back to step (1) and start over.

But don't be a fanatic. Sometimes the most productive thing you can do at a given moment is to sit down with your favourite person and spend an hour watching the sun go down. Sometimes the most productive thing possible will be exercising, sleeping, or taking a well-deserved vacation. And, very often, the most productive thing you can do this minute will be the last thing you want to do right now. The edge between winners and losers cuts sharpest at this precise point.

Winners almost always do what they think is the most productive thing possible at every given moment; losers almost never do. When you look at what winners and losers actually do moment by moment, the difference between these two divisions of the human race really is that small. But the results of those small differences keep adding to each other at every given moment until they reach a critical size. Then they start multiplying.

Compare the achievements that are realized over a period of time. First, look at the results obtained by anyone you know who is doing the most productive thing possible with most of his or her moments. Then look at the results obtained by all the people you know who'll do what's easiest rather than what's most productive every chance they get.

You'll see an enormous difference. What's been accumulated and multiplied by many moments spent productively will be knowledge, skill, health, contacts, opportunities – and at least the beginnings of wealth. What's been accumulated and multiplied by many moments given to doing the easiest thing possible? Perhaps some debt for pleasures consumed and forgotten, some extra pounds around the middle, and some time moved from one's future to one's past – little or nothing of value will be retained.

We live moment by moment, not year by year. Do the most productive thing you can think of with each and every moment as you live it and your future is assured. Do that all day every working day and your progress will soon astound everyone who knows you. More importantly, you'll be astounded, delighted – and justifiably proud of yourself.

Within minutes after you dedicate yourself to this plan and put it to work, you'll notice the difference. (If you don't notice a difference right away, there are two likely explanations: (1) you're not really facing up to what is the most productive thing you can do with *this* moment; (2) you're going to put this plan to work all right – first thing on the sixth Saturday of September.)

Within hours after you make this plan yours and start doing the most productive thing possible with every given moment, you'll project a new aura of confidence and capability. Within days, people near you will sense the difference and start upgrading their opinions about your abilities and prospects. Within weeks, you'll be reaping substantial rewards from your new willingness to pay the price of success. Within months, you'll be living on a higher level than you now believe you can achieve in so short a time.

On the road to that happy result, there'll be some painful moments. There'll be times when you'll talk yourself out of doing the most productive thing – times, in other words, when you'll succeed in bringing home a failure when you could just as well have succeeded in bringing home a success. There'll be times when you'll curse the day you decided to demand so much of yourself. As you pass through some particularly low points on your road to success (make no mistake about it, you will – we all do) there'll be times when you'll lie to yourself to get out of tackling the most productive challenge facing you. Worse yet, there'll be times when you'll know you're lying to yourself but you'll still let yourself be defeated by those lies. And there'll be times when you won't be able to make yourself do anything even faintly productive.

That's the bad news.

The good news is that none of the above matters.

These little backslides don't stop you, they merely put a few extra hours between you and your goals. Shrug these minor incidents off. Resolve to do better. Then go on.

There's a technique to this. Don't destroy your fragile new confidence in yourself by demanding total dedication. Keep your balance. You need a certain level of recreation to maintain your forward thrust. Accept that fact. Resolve to enjoy a reasonable amount of earned recreation, not only because it's a highly productive use of your time, but for itself. Learn how to reward yourself for jobs well done.

If you've been self-indulgent, if you've made it a rule to do whatever you feel like doing all your life long, don't expect to completely change your performance overnight. Possessing the ability to do the most productive thing possible at most given moments requires a high degree of self-discipline. Such qualities don't become part of your personality merely from a snap decision. If you want to own this stupendous asset, there's only one way to acquire it – you must patiently build it moment by moment and day by day over a period of time. But, no matter how soft you've been with yourself, you can acquire this power if you choose to. It will merely take more time, patience, and determination to keep trying if you haven't exercised your self-disciplinary muscles much in the past.

When you realize that you've failed to do the most productive thing possible at some especially crucial moment, move aggressively to limit the damage. As you do that, also limit the damage to your self-confidence. The temptation is to feel guilty. You want to tell yourself that you're a bum, that you'll never make it, that you're a failure. After a misstep of any kind, don't chew on yourself. Never cut yourself down.

First, tell yourself that what happened will probably be worth it in the long run – that obviously you need more convincing on the importance of doing the most productive thing at every given moment. Then tell yourself, 'It's not like me to mess up like that. I'll do better next time.'

In the beginning, you may have a problem believing that. Eliminate this problem by focusing your mind on the concept that you're talking about the person you're becoming, not the person you are today. But never say, 'Someday it won't be like me to mess up that way.' The technique that works is to put superior performance in the here and now. You are who you think you are, so begin thinking that you are who you want to be. Start doing that right now – this very instant.

Because if you'll accept the fact that the main limit on your future is how fully you apply The Golden Dozen, you'll keep coming back to it in spite of occasional backsliding. Go into living the dozen with this foreknowledge: You'll find some gaps in your resolve from time to time, and along the way to large achievements you'll have to accept many small defeats.

But you'll also be winning many small victories, and an occasional big one. As time goes on and you continue to apply this plan with steady determination, you'll discover that it gets easier and easier. While that's happening, you're changing and growing far more than you may realize. As your new habit is becoming part of your personality, you'll find yourself just naturally doing the most productive thing possible during more and more moments – without strain, without driving yourself – because it's what you want to do. The time will come when selecting and doing the most productive thing will be so natural that it's almost effortless.

Once you've tasted what living by this credo can do for your life, you'll find yourself quickly shaking off every temporary lapse of determination. After every slip, you'll immediately review your reasons for wanting success. You'll reaffirm your dedication to doing what you know you must do to achieve that success. Then you'll push your engines back up to maximum thrust again by putting that moment, that hour, and the rest of the day to the most productive use possible.

No secret, no skill, and no method can be as valuable to you as the firm and constant application of the Hopkins Golden Twelve. No lucky break, no inherited advantage, and no found opportunity can for very long balance your failure to consistently do the most productive thing possible with every given moment.

Since it creates a dramatic effect after only a few days, imagine what the total cumulative result will be after you have lived by this credo for several years. I know what will happen. The Golden Twelve *can* revolutionize your life. It *can* send your accomplishments, happiness, and career soaring. It *will* do all these things if you'll apply it moment after moment, hour after hour, and day after day. How do I know it will?

Because that's what The Golden Twelve did – and is doing – for me.

3 Before you spend several years hunting for success, spend a few minutes defining it

At the age of six, Corinne Archer* started putting in long hours training. Long before she entered her teens, she had fixed her mind on a single goal: to win an Olympic gold medal. From then on, she crushed everything out of her life that didn't contribute to her goal. Every available hour went into practice. Trophies and honours piled up as the years went by, but they meant little to Corinne beyond making her dreams of winning the gold medal seem a little more real.

After eleven years, the big day finally came, and Corinne Archer arrived at the Olympics to meet the world's toughest competitors. The contest was gruelling, but she won. At seventeen, Corinne stood at the highest pinnacle she could ever hope to attain by her own definition of success. The gold medal, whose pursuit had dominated two-thirds of this young woman's life, was now hers.

Corinne left the victory stand in tears – of joy, everyone thought. But for days she was near tears much of the time. Hardly able to remember a time when every waking moment hadn't been driven by the demands of her almost impossible quest, Corinne realized almost at the instant of victory that she faced a blank future. Without that quest, this intensely goal-oriented young lady no longer had a purpose in life. From always living in the future, Corinne was suddenly thrown into living in the past.

Slowly, painfully, several difficult months went by. Then Corinne Archer began to recover from the tremendous emotional shock of losing her one goal by winning it. As she learned to live in the present, Corinne renewed her interest in life by discovering the power and beauty of having many goals rather than just one all-encompassing commitment.

Success, then, is not a thing we win, a place we arrive at, a record we set. It's not the numbers in our bank book, the address

* Although the name has been changed, this is a true story.

we live at, the position we hold. If success is none of these things, what is it?

SUCCESS IS THE CONTINUOUS JOURNEY TOWARDS THE ACHIEVEMENT OF PREDETERMINED, WORTHWHILE GOALS.

Since our lives are realities that go on and on, true success, the kind that doesn't crumble into dust the moment we get our hands on it, must be part of the continuous journey. Bend your efforts towards achieving a successful life. Only you can define precisely what achieving a successful life means to you. But, if happiness has any place in your set of values, your successful life will probe many interests, experience many emotions, fill many needs, and accomplish many aims.

Choose specific goals. Predetermine them far enough in advance of their deadlines to allow you to change and develop enough to reach them. Unless you do both these things, success will always be a stranger – or at best, a fickle, unfriendly, and infrequent visitor – at your house.

Nothing that will give lasting satisfaction can be achieved unless the goals striven for are worthwhile. Discovering and moving towards what is truly worthwhile to you is the most challenging and rewarding task of your continuous journey through life. If you would be truly successful, accept this challenge. Think about it deeply. Then act on your conclusions.

Success isn't all of a sudden – success is every day. Once you get near your current goals, start thinking about where you'll go after you get there. This is vital. And you can do it without diverting energy from nailing down the great success you're closing in on now. Before achieving that aim, rest your mind occasionally by speculating on what your next goals will be. Make a written list of your ideas. As you find free moments, collect your thoughts about your new goals. Gather information on them.

Prepare for the trauma of success. Unless you plunge into the pursuit of new goals, you'll get bored, you'll get depressed, and you'll start sliding downhill as soon as you lose the challenge of chasing your current goals. Achieving a great and long-sought success is like catching a virulent disease. This analogy isn't far-fetched – witness the number of people who win celebrity and wealth in show business and then lose everything to alcohol or drugs.

Fortunately, a solid new goal is a sure cure. Don't leave your old goal without one.

4   Work smarter, not harder – uh-huh

One of the most dangerous ideas around is stated by only four words: 'Work smarter, not harder.' The danger in this saying comes from the fact that there's an enormous amount of truth in it.

The problem is, the truth it expresses isn't the whole truth. If you're going to achieve more than a small fraction of your potential, you still have to put in a great amount of effective hard work while you're working smarter. But this doesn't mean that you can't enjoy your work. In fact, most of the really smart, effective, and highly-rewarded work is done by individuals who love what they're doing.

People frequently tell me they work smarter, not harder. But, in almost every case where I've known one of these people well enough to understand his action, I find that they aren't really working smarter, not harder. What they're actually doing is shortcutting, avoiding reality, and playing games. A large part of their energy – and a tremendous amount of hard work – goes into frantic manoeuvres to avoid the consequences of their own smartness.

At the other end of the stick are the ones who drive themselves with such intensity that they never act on – or even see – any opportunity or problem that's developing outside the tunnel they're digging. Their concentration on hard work keeps them from adjusting to changes in the rapidly evolving culture and economy we live in. All too often, the changes rising beyond their vision will rob them of the fruits of their labours.

Let's revise that four-word saying, and go with a slightly longer one that's a far more reliable guide to success:

WORK SMARTER – AND AS HARD AS YOU CAN WITHOUT SACRIFICING ALERTNESS.

5 No one can give you what they don't have

How many times have you sat in a classroom in front of a teacher or professor who never left school?

Most educators have never faced the realities of the market-place, have never risked everything to start something, have never operated a business, have never had the responsibility of making a profit in order to keep people on the payroll – have never, in other words, made much money.

Can these security-minded educators teach you how to pay the price of success?

Let's consider your friends. Some of them never exert them-selves. They aspire to nothing much, and spend their years watching instead of doing. These people haven't paid, and never will pay, much of a price, so they haven't achieved, and never will achieve, much of a success. Can they give you help, good advice, and emotional support towards achieving your goals?

Let's press into even more sensitive territory. (Please bear with me. I wouldn't do this if it wasn't important.)

Do you aspire to achieve more than your parents have achieved?

For example, let's say that your goal is to be a millionaire. This is a fine goal. Money is good if the money you earn is in direct proportion to the services you give other people. However, if your parents are not millionaires, can they give you the skills, know-ledge, and guidance you need to become a millionaire?

Your teachers, your friends, and your parents certainly all want the best for you. Their motives are good, their intentions are good. But they see the world through the curtain of their own faults, fears, and failures. Like all humans, they are guided by their feelings. They are *for* what is familiar to them, *against* what is not.

If you turn to them for advice, what can they give you? Their experience, which is not what you want to repeat.

**NO ONE CAN TEACH YOU THAT WHICH THEY
HAVE NOT DONE.**

No matter what we want to do, many aspects of our goals have been achieved by others before us. Much of our accomplishments will always be a recombination and repetition of things already done. What does this mean? That we can learn more from the experience of others than we have time on this earth to discover for ourselves. Find a way to learn from those who have already been where you want to go. Trust their experience above those who haven't done what you want to do.

And always, put your ultimate trust in yourself.

6   Grasp the essence of leadership

There are a few kinds of success that don't require leadership. A very few. Unless you're convinced that you'll never need to display leadership, miss no opportunity to develop it.

What is the essence of leadership? The ability to make your followers believe that you possess superior knowledge of the situation, greater wisdom to cope with the unknown, or greater moral force. Unless you seem to have more of these things than the average follower does, they won't follow you around the first corner.

Superior knowledge of the specific situation you're involved with must be acquired on the scene. Greater wisdom comes from study that's tested by experience. Although moral force is also a learned quality, it springs from an inner commitment to greatness that any of us can make. One of the best examples is an incident in the life of Alexander.

Three hundred years before our era, Alexander the Great led a forced march across a hot and desolate plain. On the eleventh day, he and all the soldiers still with him were near death from thirst. Alexander pressed on. At midday, two scouts brought him what little water they had been able to find – it hardly filled the bottom of a helmet. Their throats burning, Alexander's men stood back and watched him enviously. Alexander didn't hesitate. He turned the helmet over and poured the water on the hot sand at his feet. Then he said, 'It's of no use for one to drink when many thirst.' They desperately needed water – quantities of it – when Alexander had but a few drops. So he gave them the only thing he did have: inspiration.

That's leadership.

7 Fix on a great aim beyond the major goal you're seeking now

Jonas Salk's great aim wasn't to become head of the lab so he could qualify for a pension. He set his sights on conquering polio.

If your great aim is to move up a notch, your immediate superior will find it easy not to think about you. If your great aim is to be his boss, he'll find it hard not to trip you up.

What happens when your action indicates that you'll achieve some great aim within a few years, such as becoming a divisional vice-president six levels above your present supervisor? That is, if you make your immediate superior feel the pressure of your tomorrow – without arrogance, without making an enemy – what will happen today?

Your talents will be more quickly recognized. Opportunities will be more readily found for you. Everybody likes to go with a winner.

That's one of the smaller benefits you'll derive from having a great aim beyond the major goal you're seeking now. A greater benefit is the vastly improved perspective you'll have of the obstacles and problems you're encountering today. All too often, we look at our present problems as though they were mountains looming over us that must be climbed one step at a time.

Looking down from the vantage point of your great aim, these present difficulties are clearly seen as the minor inconveniences they really are. From that same elevated vantage point, you'll find it easier to set your targets higher, to demand more of yourself, and to accept more rejection and more failure without becoming discouraged and quitting. You'll find it easier to endure today's trials when you understand clearly how essential they are to prepare you for the great goal of your future.

8 Make your great aims realistic before you admit to them

Don't tell the world you're going to be the chairman of the board when there's doubt that you can cut it in the mail room. Snickers don't help. A blowhard reputation doesn't help. What helps is racking up rows of success-building performances at whatever you're doing now.

That calls for more than keeping your shoes shined, showing up on time, and meeting the quota. A success-building performance is one that worries the weak and inspires the strong.

As soon as you realize you're doing that, quietly make the people a level or two above you aware that they have nothing to fear from you. You're not after their job – you're aiming much higher.

9 Create a sensation, then talk to the top

Do something impressive at your job. Not something offbeat, but something that's sensationally helpful in the direction your management wants to go. For example, when almost no one is even meeting it, consistently turn in 200% or more of the quota.

Impossible? Not at all – assuming that you're not working in a depressed industry or for a non-competitive company. (If you are, why? Inertia? Go where the action is.)

The point is to gain access to the people on top. Until they know you, they can't help you.

Be realistic. If your immediate boss is insecure, turning in a sensational performance may give that person nightmares. In this case, your terrific performance may be downplayed, or even concealed. When things like this happen, go over that person's head. If that doesn't work, take your skills, knowledge, and energy elsewhere.

10   Green grassers and mountain climbers

Most of us have acquaintances or relatives who change jobs frequently. Many of these people work hard, appear to be capable, and always seem on the verge of hitting something big. But they never do. Take a close look at what they're accomplishing by jumping from one field to another in search of greener grass. From what they tell you is a poor opportunity, they'll hop to what they tell you is a better one. You think they're all set. Next you hear that the new patch of grass isn't so green after all. Pretty soon, they're off again to another greener-looking pasture.

You probably also know a few other people who are steadily climbing towards a distant peak. Their efforts don't always take them higher, but all of them are made with reason to believe they will. Purpose and continuity are woven into all their actions. Whenever the way ahead is blocked, they search out new routes that'll take them up. They never lose sight of the mountain top they've chosen. Since they've chosen the goal with great care, and with the knowledge that the climb to it will be long and difficult, they are a mountain of determination. These people are climbing, not wandering.

Green grassers don't realize that making anything grow takes persistence and hard work. What they're really looking for is a soft touch – a long success from a short effort – but there's no such thing. So the green grassers waste their lives searching for something that doesn't exist.

Learn the difference between green grassers and mountain climbers. Then make sure you spend more time with the type you want to be and less time with the type you don't want to be.

11   How to guarantee that you'll never meet your quota

It's really easy to organize yourself so that you'll never run any risk of meeting your quota – which is why so many people do this. All you have to do is set your sights on meeting the quota.

How's that again?

What I'm saying is this: if all you try to do is meet the quota, you'll never do it.

Why not?

Because you'll organize your activity to achieve the quota – which means barely meeting it. Something will always go wrong with part of your action, resulting in at least a small shortfall. 'Had it in the bag. Then Jasper Jones fell apart on me. If it wasn't for that fink Jones, I'd have made it easy.'

If you're aiming to be average, this gets you there okay. But if you're aiming higher, this is nowhere.

Begin by organizing your activity so that you can double the quota. This way, when Bart bounces a check, Carl cancels an order, and Dave delays a bid, you'll still do well with what's left. When you start hitting 200% of quota, bump your goal to 300%.

Don't meet any quota that's set for ordinary people – demolish it.

12   The art of making enemies

It's amazing how many people make enemies in situations where they gain no advantage by doing so. There are so many times when all it takes to ease a shock is a friendly word. The mark of the true Champion is that he or she takes a moment to find a way to be a good winner who leaves respect behind, instead of being a poor winner who leaves hate behind.

There are times when you must say no, when you must block someone's move, when it's you or them. But if you concentrate on achieving your goal – not on preventing others from achieving theirs – you can often win big without creating even a little enmity. Respect your adversaries, respect your competition, respect your fellow human. Almost everybody accepts losing to someone who fights hard but clean, someone who can win without arrogance, someone who clearly has earned his or her victory.

Don't chop the other guy's liver any finer than you have to. The future is an enigma. None of us can be certain that we'll never need something from a former boss, competitor, co-worker, customer, employee, neighbour, supplier, or anyone at all whom we've had contact with. That something might be a recommendation, a crucial vote, an order, or a vital bit of information. It might even be your job.

Not long ago, a department head in a small city was ordered by the city manager to fire one of his employees. It was a distasteful task to the department head, so he handled the matter quickly, without giving any consideration to how the blow might be eased, or trying to get the order reversed. This treatment was highly motivating to the fired employee. He ran for the city council and was elected. Once in office, it was a simple matter for the ex-employee to trade his council vote on other matters for support on his chief aim: firing the two men who had fired him a few weeks before. The department head then found himself out of work at a time when positions in his speciality were very tight. The best job he could find was in another field where he had to take a large pay cut. Always keep in mind that the enemy you avoid making today may control something that's very important to you tomorrow.

Don't make enemies for free.

13   Stop thinking 'if only' and you won't need to

'If only I could get a better break.'
'If only I had some money.'
'If only I would've married the right person.'

'If only I worked for the right company.'
'If only I had the right parents.'

Do you pull back from taking full personal responsibility for yourself? Many of us do. We think that a parent, a teacher, a friend, a boss, a spouse, the company we work for, or some governmental programme should shoulder our burden for turning our lives into what we want them to be. This approach can't get the job done. Other people and organizations have too many pressing problems and priorities of their own.

What does this mean? That you'll always be disappointed when you depend on others for the things you must do for yourself. It's so easy to justify the temptation of freeloading, to slide into being a follower, to fail to see the hidden price tag in the handout. Unless you take complete control of your life and assume full personal responsibility for yourself, who will?

No one will.

Every dollar you earn is worth ten given to you. Earned money creates the self-image of self-reliance; given money creates the self-image of other-dependence. This is why some families stay on welfare for generations. Hangers-on and free-loaders are the most frustrated people on earth because they have created their own frustrations. You can't be successful and happy until you earn the respect of the toughest, hardest to fool, and most important judge in the world: yourself.

SELF-INSTRUCTION:

'I take full responsibility for my actions, and for my life. My well-being is in the best hands it could possibly be in: my own.'

14   Here is the greatest treasure you can ever own

What is it?
Before you waste time trying to choose between health, wealth,

youth, and good looks, let me tell you. The most valuable thing you can ever own is your image of yourself as a winner in the great game of life, as a contributor to the betterment of humankind, as an achiever of worthy goals. Unless you have that image of yourself, nothing worth having will stay with you for long.

SELF-INSTRUCTION:

'I am a winner. I am a contributor. I am an achiever. I believe in me.'

15   Why self-instructions work – how you can stop smoking or do anything else you want to do

Research has discovered that it takes four to ten repetitions of a thought pattern to create a seed that will grow into action. Let's say that you accept an invitation to spend the weekend water-skiing. The inboard engine on your friend's boat has no cover. He warns you about it but you forget, accidentally press your leg against the engine, and get burned. Your friend's warning didn't register, but the second one – a blister on your leg – did. After that, you'll keep your bare skin away from that engine's hot metal for the rest of the day.

One effective input – or was it just one? Actually, every time you get near the engine, a highly emotional thought pattern will flash through your mind: 'Touching the engine *hurts*.' This thought pattern is a self-instruction.

Every time you rub the burn on your leg that night, you'll get another repetition of the same thought pattern. When you go water-skiing the second day, you'll remember to keep your bare arms and legs away from that engine.

Most people limit themselves to self-instructions of this sort, the ones that chance imposes on them as they plod through life. Since the most powerful of these self-instructions are painful memories, most people are reluctant to try new things. Their minds are shot through with variations of, 'You better not try that or you'll be sorry.'

Putting it another way, the average person is governed by the experiences that get programmed into his subconscious mind beginning on day one of his life. He does little or nothing to influence those programmes, and accepts their rule without question. The more haphazard and negative his experiences are, the more power they will have to encourage negative behaviour and discourage positive effort.

Every successful person, on the other hand, has some understanding of self-instructions, and uses positive thought patterns to create effective action. These are the people who say, 'I can do that.' Then they do it.

Higher achievers go further. They use self-instructions in an organized and consistent way to get what they want from life. If you're not on an organized and consistent programme to multiply your achievements with positive self-instructions, what are you waiting for? When you finish this, reread section 1 and get started.

Some people deny that self-instructions work – but they still use them every day of their lives. They can't help themselves because we all talk to ourselves most of the time. Only a special elite of highly successful people are wise enough to use this powerful flow of images and ideas in a positive and regular manner. You can join this elite today.

Self-instructions are deliberately repeated thoughts about yourself that you have decided to make come true. *They are not true when you begin to use them.* If they were true now, there'd be no need to consciously repeat them because you're already repeating them unconsciously often enough to make them, and keep them, true.

Let's suppose that you have decided to stop smoking. I'm not suggesting that you quit. When I smoked – as I did for years – I didn't want anyone telling me to stop. Then I decided to quit. Using this method, there was nothing to it. If you want to keep on smoking, be my guest. Learn this method anyway – then use it to grasp every achievable goal that you do desire.

For the moment then, let's say that you are a smoker who's

decided to give it up. You don't really want to – the truth is, you like to smoke. In your mind, smoking is you – macho, sexy, devil-may-care, elegant, whatever. But you want to start giving a higher priority to your health. So you say, 'I'm going to quit.'

Three months later you're smoking more than you ever did; you're sick of feeling guilty about smoking; and you're tired of fighting yourself about it. Yet you still want to quit. But you haven't. What happened?

You never had a chance of quitting because you kept on instructing yourself that you are a smoker. 'Yeah, I'd like to quit, but, uh – I just can't. You know, I really like a cigarette with a cup of coffee, and – ' These are self-instructions. Constantly repeated, they are unbeatable – except by other self-instructions. Fight fire with fire. Here's how:

1. Give a few moments' thought to why you smoke. Did you start when you were a kid because it made you feel like a big deal? Whatever your emotional reasons were for starting six or sixty years ago, that seed is still creating action today. Don't linger over this step. Take a stab at the reason and go on.

2. Write out a self-instruction that attacks the habit you want to change and the reason behind it as directly and *as emotionally* as possible. Perhaps you don't have a clue to the real reason why you're doing, or not doing, whatever it is that you want to change. Then develop instructions that go right to the heart of the matter. Again, pack as much emotion as you can into your words. Lay it on about how great you'll feel when you're enjoying what you're seeking. Dwell on the worst problems you'll avoid. Most people produce their most emotional and effective self-instructions by saying what they think out loud and then writing their strongest thoughts down.

If you're a smoker who wants to keep on smoking, don't let the direct language below upset you. The point here is to learn how to apply this method to whatever you want to achieve. As you study the method, remember that the harder you hit your gut emotions, the quicker you'll achieve the purpose you've chosen. To stop smoking, your positive new thought pattern might go something like this:

SELF-INSTRUCTIONS:

'No one but an (*choose your own expletive*) would smoke. Every time I see somebody light up a killer weed, I know I'm looking at a dumb jerk. I hate cigarettes. They stink. Tobacco makes your mouth taste like a highway toilet. But the worst part is how much crud they were putting in my body. Can you believe it, I was actually paying for stuff that was constricting my capillaries and wearing my heart out by making it work harder. Not only that, I was running a terrible risk of throat and lung cancer, and I was wheezing and coughing all the time. Who knows all the ways that cigarettes were killing me? Only an idiot would smoke, and I'm no idiot. Hurray for me – I've quit smoking!

'It was easy. I just threw the damn things away and stopped. No stupid habit like that is ever going to control me. When I decide to quit something, that's it – I quit. End of habit.

'I'm done with paying out good money for something that was digging my grave. I'm proud of myself for quitting, and I sure feel great since I did. I've got more energy, more wind, and I feel more alive. It's great to know that I'm not offending people by blowing smoke and cigarette breath at them anymore. There's no way I'd ever touch one of those rotten things again.'

3. Whatever personal habit you want to change, write a self-instruction that's as emotional as the one you just read. Be sure to use words that say, 'I've already done it. This is the new me, and am I glad!' In a moment I'll show you why the only effective self-instruction is the 'I've already done it' kind. Please realize that if you cast your achievement desires into the future with 'I'm going to' phrases, you'll kill your goals in their eggs. 'I'm going to' simply expresses a wish, and wishes never change anything.

4. Review your self-instructions in the morning; review them at least once during the day; review them again at bedtime. The key to making them create the new person you want to be is to get yourself to really feel the emotions of each instruction as you read it. The emotions are the motors that power the changes you want

to make happen – the keener you make yourself feel those emotions, the quicker they'll do their work.

Don't be discouraged if you don't feel the emotions very strongly at first. Keep trying. They will start welling up in you as soon as you master the little trick of mentally putting yourself where you want to be for an instant. As you do this, be sure to look at the world through your own eyes – don't mentally float overhead and watch yourself. Effective self-instruction happens when you feel the reality you want to create, not when you daydream about it.

5. Don't fight yourself about changing. Do just what you want to do. As long as you keep on reviewing your self-instructions three times a day, taking a few moments each time to really feel their emotions, you're reprogramming yourself. If you continue with this, your actions have to change.

Returning to the example of the smoker who wants to quit, he will soon realize that he can't emotionalize the 'I've quit' statement given above three times a day and also keep on smoking. If you are a smoker who wants to stop, I challenge you to give this system a full and willing trial. I don't guarantee that you'll quit smoking. All I guarantee is that you'll quit smoking within 21 days or you'll quit reviewing and emotionalizing the above instruction.

Before you can turn off any major habit such as smoking, you have to make some changes in how you feel about yourself and the world around you. The instructions will cause that to happen – if you want it to. If you don't, you will quit reviewing the instruction as soon as you realize that it's going to work. You see, you really will quit smoking if you keep on reviewing a self-instruction that says you already have quit in powerful emotional terms that also make powerful common sense. Why? Because you just can't keep on lying to yourself that plainly for 21 days.

That's why it works.

16   Use your self-instructions to control other people

The highest achievers use their self-instructions so spectacularly that they exert as powerful an influence on others as they do on themselves. To do this, you create a self-instruction about a success you will achieve that involves someone else. Then reach everybody you can with it: deliver that self-instruction loudly, sensationally, and often. The more outrageous humour you put in your message, the harder it hits.

This method can work with one person or on a group. But it can't be generalized. To be effective, your message has to be aimed at a specific person or group. He, she, or they must be made keenly aware of it. And your message has to be aimed at winning a specific success for yourself. Your success might require that the other person or group lose a contest, or it might mean that you all accomplish something together. However, it won't work if what you're doing is nagging or propagandizing for someone else's success, as parents discover every time they try this on their children.

Muhammad Ali was one of the world's most brilliant practitioners of this technique. The record of his heavyweight boxing career is crowded with examples of this 'master of mind control' defeating his opponents mentally before they climbed in the ring with him. Along with superb athletic abilities, Ali was a genius at psychological warfare. 'The bear will fall in five,' he chanted over and over. Everyone except the bear laughed at Ali's boasts and rhymes in the weeks prior to the fight. But the bear heard them – over and over and over. Doubt crept into his mind, and then grew faster and faster. When the time came, the bear fell in five rounds exactly as Ali had convinced him he would.

17   Self-instruct yourself to be healthy

For years, the realization has been growing among medical researchers that, *without exception*, your health is heavily influenced by the instructions you give yourself. This means that, without exception, how severely any disease will affect you is largely decided by what you have told yourself about your life.

In other words, the happier you are about yourself and your life, the healthier you will be. It's never too late to change. Even many longstanding conditions have responded amazingly well when people start telling themselves that they feel great about living.

SELF-INSTRUCTION:

'I'm wonderfully healthy. All my organs are working perfectly. I'm healthy for seven reasons: I'm happy. I love my life. I'm always discovering fascinating new things to do. I know that I have a wonderful future. I don't put anything except good stuff in my mind and body. I exercise regularly and wisely. And I stay out of the way of fast-moving objects.'

18   Make the most powerful word in the language work for you

The most powerful word in the English language is *balance*. Work hard. That's fine. Then balance your hard work with hard play. Thousands of the most effective people maintain a state of balance that allows them to increase their mental and physical health and increase their earning power at the same time. Their secret is that they stay loose and relaxed as they work all out – and then they devote all-out time to quality recreation.

Some high-achievers balance hard work with hard play on a daily basis. If you have the strength of mind to manage it, this is the best method. When you're earning lots of money doing something you love doing, it isn't easy to make yourself walk away from all that excitement every day for something as intangible as maintaining balance. For most high achievers, doing this requires a far higher order of self-discipline than losing themselves in their work.

Keeping your balance on a daily basis means that you must put non-work commitments ahead of work commitments for part of every day. There's no way around this. Whether it's being with your family, working out at the gym, meeting your spiritual needs, attending an event with a child, or enjoying a hobby, whatever lets you maintain your equilibrium must become your number one priority during the hours you assign to it.

Doubling up on activities helps. Have your son ride his bike along with you as you jog; take your spouse on working trips; meet for lunch; take one of your children with you when you're out making calls; reprogramme your mind and schedule so that you can work effectively at home a few weekdays a month. There are ways to be with your family more often if you'll use your ingenuity to find them. Keep at it. The penalties for losing equilibrium with your family can quickly cancel out everything you've earned for them by working too hard too long.

It's so easy to let your life get out of balance. A new development or insight excites you and, before you know it, you're running flat out. That's my problem. I get an idea about taking a new direction and suddenly it's all-consuming. Before I know it, I'm putting in seven days a week again; I'm hitting it fifteen or sixteen hours a day again – and I'm loving every minute. But, inside me and around me, difficulties are sprouting like weeds, and small problems are rapidly turning into heaps of trouble.

I can coach you here because I've been out of balance many times. Every time I slip out of balance, one of two things always happens: (a) I recognize what's going on quickly and push my life back into balance before any serious damage is done. (b) I stay out of balance too long and have penalties to pay before I can get myself back into balance.

My experiences with losing equilibrium aren't unique – this is a universal problem. It can afflict anyone because there are as many ways to fall out of balance as there are things to do. You're out of balance when your clothes don't fit around the waist anymore, when you start dealing with today's problems by drinking yourself into tomorrow's hangover, when you bet the rent money at the dog races, when you don't like yourself.

You're out of balance when you can't say, 'I was wrong;' when you won't say, 'I love you;' when you don't say, 'Let's work this out.' You're out of balance when you can't hug your kids because you're working seventy hours a week. You're out of balance when you're not working effectively, when you can't laugh at yourself, when you don't feel worthy of respect.

If you stay out of balance long enough – sometimes it doesn't take long at all – you'll always run into trouble. This trouble can take many forms, it can be very severe, and you rarely have any choice about what kind of trouble will hit you.

Unfortunately, getting into trouble doesn't automatically mean that you'll be rocked back into balance. More often than not, paying one penalty for being out of balance simply lines you up for a repeat performance, or leads you to another form of imbalance.

Throughout our lives all of us must punch the time clock at the business of keeping our physical and emotional equilibrium intact, just to survive, first of all. Secondly, before we're capable of delivering a superior performance for more than a few months, we have to get into balance within ourselves and stay that way. No one can do this for you. Before you can have balance, you must want it. And you must be willing to pay for it with some of the precious stuff called time.

How is this balance achieved and maintained?

By going on a positive mental diet. To control your life so that you can do what you choose with it, control your thoughts. If you want to have a positive life, feed your mind positive food; if you want to live a junky life, feed your mind junk. Only you can decide what food your mind will feed on; only you can make your decision stick.

What is a positive mental diet?

It's reading good books, hearing good tapes, and associating with effective people. Keep a positive book on your bedstand and read a good thing or two each night before you go to sleep. Put a cassette player in your bathroom and listen to positive voices while you get ready in the morning. Mix in some energetic music that makes you feel good, music that puts you in the mood to have an enthusiastic and effective day. Choose your friends and associates carefully so that you'll be charging forward with positive people instead of sprinting backwards with negative people.

Do these things work? Do they really make any difference? Let me tell you: they make all the difference. I know because I've been doing them for years. That's right – I read positive books; I listen to positive tapes and upbeat music; I seek out positive people and avoid negative people.

And I don't let the media use my head for a septic tank. To sum it up, I'm careful about what I read, listen to, and watch. Calamities, corruption and crime sell more newspapers and commercials than good news does. The average person is comforted by hearing about other people's troubles, and fear is a more compelling emotion than confidence to the person who doesn't control his or her thoughts. If you would be successful, see to it that confidence is more compelling, exciting, and comforting to you than fear. There is no other way to attain your goals.

Fear is more addictive, more easily packaged, and more easily sold than any other emotion, which is why it's the most profitable commodity the news media has. If you let yourself become addicted to a daily dose of dismal details about events beyond your control, how can you be confident about your own prospects? How can you jump out of bed brimming with enthusiasm when the last food you fed your mind before going to bed was the evening news? That's one of the worst negative inputs you can legally get. Don't self-instruct yourself on all the catastrophes and violence in the world 365 yimes a year and then expect your subconscious mind to help you achieve good things. If you put rubbish, fear, and disaster into your subconscious mind, what do you think will spill out of it all over your goals, actions, and dreams? That's right – rubbish, fear, and disaster.

Make sure that everything you say to yourself is part of a continuous flow of positive thought. This doesn't mean that you avoid coping with the genuine problems that really do concern you – just the opposite. It means that you'll approach those problems in a positive, realistic, and solution-minded manner. And it also means that you'll tune out all the bad news from afar that you can't do anything about.

How can you speed up this process and make a positive mental diet bring you to the success of your choice faster?

Repeat positive new self-instructions to yourself *with keen emotional intensity* as often as you can. This is the most effective way I know of to add speed, power, and control to your drive for success. One of the finest self-instructions ever conceived is short and simple, but it'll improve your percentage in thousands of situations. It's the last one given below.

SELF-INSTRUCTIONS:

'I read something positive every night and listen to something helpful every morning.'

'I avoid negative people and negative input from the media. When someone tries to dump some negative thinking on me, I refuse to accept it.'

'I always welcome positive new ideas.'

'It's amazing how often I meet interesting new people who have an enthusiastic outlook.'

'I never carelessly spend my time with negative people.'

'I update my self-instructions once a month and review them three times a day.'

'I can do that.'

19 Losers fight, winners fly

At the most basic level, only two responses are possible to every challenge. This is also true of every opportunity. In fact, it applies to every kind of situation. You can only fight or not fight.

Doing nothing is often the best possible way to handle a situation. This is why winners do nothing in response to petty irritations and provocations so much more often than losers do. Winners have time for useful discussion but none for useless argument – they don't bother defending things that need no defence. They never risk everything where they can gain nothing, which is something losers often do.

This is not to say that winners always fly away from hard situations. When important things are at stake and it's necessary that they fight, look out – they're smart, tough, and effective. The rest of the time, the winners happily fly high over the heads of the quick-to-squabble losers.

SELF-INSTRUCTIONS:

'I respect myself and my future too much to waste energy proving things that don't matter. I don't need to. But when my vital interests really are at stake, I'm a smart, resourceful, tough fighter – and I win.'

20 How to dispose of your anger before it flushes you down the drain

We know that it's dangerous to hold anger inside ourselves for long periods of time. But if we're not going to fight, how are we going to get rid of it?

The answer is simple, easy, and it always works: the best flush for hot anger is hot sweat. When you're mad at someone or about something, before you lash out with unwise words or actions, exercise until your anger is gone. Then, with your mind cool, decide what, if anything, you should say or do.

If you're not in good physical condition, be careful while you're sweating your anger away. Instead of running your anger off, walk it off, pound a pillow, or kick something (not someone) that's soft. If you're in great shape, let your anger out with impact exercise. Have a practice session by yourself in a handball or racquetball court and slam the ball around until whatever is bothering you has lost its sharp edge. When you walk on the court to get rid of anger, don't play a game with someone – the last thing you need is the aggravation of losing because you're too upset to play well.

The best impact exercise of all is the heavy punching bag. Many gyms have both heavy and light punching bags. Avoid the light bag when you're working off anger – it'll only add to your frustration. Keep smacking the heavy bag – you can't miss it – and very soon your anger will vanish. One word of caution – don't imagine that you're punching whoever made you angry as you work on the bag – you might throw a punch at that person the next time you see him.

Psychologists have discovered that people who get a good workout regularly – runners, joggers, hikers, swimmers, weight-lifters, ball-players – don't have as many emotional problems as their flabby friends do. And the fewer emotional problems that physically-fit people do have are far more likely to be minor and under control. Those who don't exercise cut themselves off from nature's greatest mental healer – sweat.

SELF-INSTRUCTIONS:

(The first one can enormously improve the prospects of anyone who's been getting in big trouble because for years they've been telling themselves that they're hotheaded. Remember, when you backslide, you just tell yourself, 'That's not my style at all,' and go back to repeating how you want to be as though you already are that way.)

'I'm always cool. Nothing can get to me so much that I can't hold it in until I have a chance to sweat my anger away. After that I decide what, if anything, I'm going to do about the problem. I operate on the theory that there's always time to be cool and clever.'

'My emotions don't control me, I control them. I don't tense up and grit my teeth, I control my emotions by using my body and mind as one. Instead of trying to bottle up anger and stress for long periods of time, I exercise it away.'

21 Use anger as a tool

What makes anger a useful tool and when should you use it? Begin by recognizing that when you use anger on anyone, you are raising the stakes. If it is the first time that you have ever used anger on that person, you may be raising the stakes so high that the situation will turn into a different kind of game. It's much safer to motivate or influence other people calmly and firmly.

Anger is powerful medicine. Any situation that you treat with it is probably going to change fast. But, unless you understand how and on whom to use anger, your angry words are more likely to make the situation worse instead of better. Why? Because when you show anger, the other person adds a second very threatening message to what you say. That message is, 'I'm fed up – and I'm close to doing something drastic.'

Many people can't handle someone else's anger. Some automatically fly into a rage themselves. Others, especially those who feel that they are in a weak position compared to the angry person, start looking for safe ways to get revenge. In either case, the positive side of the relationship is often wrecked. When this happens, your anger has served no success-building purpose.

Anger can't be an effective tool unless your anger is justified. Make yourself stand back and look at the situation from the other person's viewpoint: is your anger reasonable under the circumstances? One of the greatest aids to making good is the ability to put yourself in the other person's shoes in all situations – but especially when you're angry. Be honest with yourself here. A quick way to destroy your prospects of success is to get the reputation of dumping the blame for your own failures onto other people.

Here's how to put legitimate anger to work at motivating or influencing another person:

1. Make sure that the two of you are alone.
Dropping your anger on another person in front of someone else is a sure way to get bad instead of good results.

2. Tell them that a serious discussion is coming up.

Say something like, 'We have a problem, and I've got to talk to you about it. When can we get together where we won't be disturbed for a while?' Quite often the other person will have some clue to what's bothering you. The announcement, by giving them time to start feeling a little anxiety, prepares them to be influenced.

3. Attack the problem, not the person.

Think about this in advance so that you can separate the results you want from the person you want them from. At first, separating personalities from problems might look difficult, or even impossible. But if you work at each situation as it comes up, you can figure out how to hit that problem with your anger without destroying the other person's self-respect. Practise this skill – all winners have it. Learn to make the people you depend on want to find ways to help you, not ways to get even with you.

4. Be precise.

Tell the other person exactly what is making you angry and exactly what he can do to eliminate the problem. And be sure to tell him in plain language that you're angry. Choose words that will get the point across. Avoid overkill. Sometimes strong language is necessary to make your message stick. More often, strong language damages or destroys the other person's desire to improve. Choose what you say and how you will say it carefully; base your decision on what will influence the other person's unique individuality, not on what will relieve your own frustrations.

5. Throw the burden on the other person.

Ask him what he's going to do about the cause of your anger. If setting a time table is appropriate, work a realistic one out. The other person must agree wholeheartedly to the schedule or he won't meet it.

6. Be as brief as possible.

If you go on and on after you've covered the matter, the other person will decide that you're simply unloading your own problems on him rather than sincerely trying to achieve anything positive.

7. Find something to praise.
As you close the meeting, show the other person that you aren't prejudiced against him by saying one good thing about some activity of his. Send him away convinced that he can and should do better, not convinced that you will be his enemy forever.

22   Use all your systems right

Art Hampson achieved his financial goals by the time he was thirty-four. So he sold his business, moved to Aspen, and plunged into the good life at that famous resort city. When an international ski race was held at Aspen a few weeks later, Art volunteered to be a gatekeeper. This involved standing on the slope for a couple of hours making sure that each racer passed between the flagged poles of the course.

Art's first day of gatekeeping dawned cold and cloudy. A stiff wind sprang up, and Art soon discovered that he was a lot colder standing around his gate than he had ever felt while actively skiing. Finally the last racer went through and Art was free to ski down to the warm lodge. Thoroughly chilled and anxious to get there as soon as possible, Art started his descent with a jump. When he landed a few feet down the slope, his chilled muscles were too stiff to share the shock, and one of Art's leg bones shattered.

Not until his third winter in Aspen was Art able to ski again. Had he warmed up his leg muscles with a few minutes of exercising in place, all would have been well.

> Use your body right: warm it up before you put it under strain. Use your mind right: psyche it up before you put it under strain.

Use every system right. If you're cold and turn the thermostat up to 90 degrees, the house won't get comfortably warm any quicker than it would had you set the temperature where you really want it. Instead, the furnace will keep on heating the house until you start sweating and turn the thermostat down again. When it's 105 outside and you come home to hot rooms, setting your air conditioner on 50 won't get the temperature down to 72 degrees any quicker than setting it on 72.

Most systems work like that – they just turn on and off. Your body has a lot of switches in it that should be flipped with care. People hear that Vitamin C is good for them, so they start taking 10,000 units a day, and train their bodies to throw off huge amounts of C. Eventually, they forget or get tired of taking the huge doses – maybe because they've heard about some other miracle pill. Their bodies keep on throwing off huge amounts of vitamin C until it's totally gone. By forgetting about the reverse effect of overdoing, the heavy C hitter causes the very thing he was trying to avoid: a vitamin deficiency severe enough to damage his health.

When you turn any system on, set the controls correctly. And don't forget to check once in a while to see whether anything needs a shot of attention or grease to keep it from tearing itself up.

SELF INSTRUCTIONS:

> 'I use all my resources right. I psyche my mind up for important activities; I warm my body up for challenges; I steer clear of overdosing and under-exercising.'

23   How to master the art of getting great ideas

After achieving his first big success, Mickey Spillane, the famous writer of detective stories, felt that he needed to work less and play more for a while. So he settled in at a popular seaside resort that summer and began having a great time.

During the long lazy days of that summer at the beach, Mickey often sat down at his typewriter to work. But the ideas just wouldn't come to this gifted young writer. With plenty of money in the bank, Mickey wasn't worried. Each time, after trying to work for a few minutes, he'd give up and go back to enjoying himself. Somehow it didn't seem important that his bank balance was steadily shrinking.

Then some unplanned expenses came up and, overnight, Mickey's financial situation changed from comfortable to uncomfortable. Keenly aware that he needed to make money fast, Mickey was at his typewriter early the next morning. For the first time in months he had determination in his heart.

But this time he *was* worried. A whole summer without a single idea worth putting on paper! Had his writing skill been baked out on the beach? Within a few minutes Spillane knew the answer. Ideas – good, salable ideas – were crowding into his mind. Under the goad of necessity he wrote one of his best stories, and then went on to the outstanding career that continues today.

How do you practise the art of getting great ideas? There are six requirements: want, need, exactness, preparation, belief, and execution.

WANT AND NEED

You won't get ideas unless you somehow tell your subconscious mind that you both need and really want ideas. The key word here is *want*. It's far more important to want ideas than to merely need them. Understanding this distinction is crucial. All constant losers, compulsive gamblers, and confirmed alcoholics desperately need new ideas to change their direction before it's too late. Since positive ideas are everywhere, why don't these people jump on some of them?

Because they don't want to stop doing what's hurting them; they don't want to pay the price of success; they don't want to face realities of living; they don't want to change.

EXACTNESS

You have to know the specific kind of solutions you want. Mickey Spillane thought of exciting scenes when he needed them because he knew exactly what he wanted – ideas for great detective stories. We all want ideas that will make us millions. Unfortunately, that's not specific enough to let the subconscious mind do its work. You can't pull important and specific ideas out of your subconscious mind until you've put important and specific problems in it.

PREPARATION

Nothing is free. Profitable innovation and effective imagination are no exception to this rule. Inventiveness and creativity aren't gifts that a lucky few use effortlessly – that notion is false. After you've paid the price, your imagination will soar and innovative ideas will flow from your brain. The price for that result has to be paid with study, with experience-gaining work, and with alert thought. You create ideas by becoming specific in your thinking and thorough with your study of a subject that excites you. Success-building ideas come only to those who look for them vigorously and intelligently.

BELIEF

Your subconscious mind wants to be used; it wants to be controlled intelligently; it wants to help you grow and win and be happy. So it will go along with self-instructions that aren't true today in order to help you make them true tomorrow.

But it won't allow you to fool it forever. In the laborious process of creating ideas, your subconscious mind has to know that some of them will be used. Not necessarily all of them – or even most of them. But a few of them must be used. Otherwise the flow will eventually be choked off. The more ideas you use and benefit from, the more ideas you'll have and the better they'll be.

EXECUTION

The profit of great ideas comes when you turn them into reality. Get rid of the delusion that you can have a great idea and then get a mechanic to work out the details. The details are the invention. Unless you work out the details in a practical way, you can't control the profit that can be made from your great idea.

Pick a limited field to specialize in. Learn everything that's already known about the subject. Work in that field by taking the best job you can find in it rather than a better one elsewhere. Then start thinking every hour of every day about what can be done to improve performance in your speciality. When you've done all these things, valuable ideas will start flowing out of your mind. Success is doing, not wishing.

SELF-INSTRUCTION:

'I am an idea person. I get a lot of great ideas because I know exactly what I want, and I keep my subconscious mind loaded with material that allows it to generate them.'

24   Don't raise frogs unless you can hear the croaking

After reading a breeder frog grower's advertisement, Pete Williams realized that raising frogs for the gourmet food market would be a sure thing and a natural way to wealth. All you need is some water and a few breeder frogs. What could be better? Free bugs are everywhere. They fly in and practically ask the frogs to eat them.

It took Pete three years to save enough money to start his frog farm. Finally, the dream started to become a reality; Pete was able to lease some suitable land. He paid for several days' work by earthmoving machines to dam a stream and scoop out a large pond. After the pond began to fill, Pete ordered several pairs of breeder frogs. When they arrived by air freight, he rushed out and popped them in the water.

After that, Pete visited his frog farm nearly every weekend. He liked to get there about sundown and listen to them croaking out their rib-it sounds. Soon the second generation added their voices to the nightly chorus. It was reassuring to realize that, as the advertisements had promised, the frogs actually were feeding themselves. Within a few months, Pete could see a big payday coming up from his frog farm.

At last, the time came to cash in on his venture. Pete gathered up all the necessary gear and drove to his lonely pond far out in the country. As Pete climbed out of his pickup truck, he realized that something was wrong: not a single croak was coming from the pond.

Within a few minutes, he found muddy footprints and tyre tracks that confirmed what had happened: someone else had harvested every one of his frogs.

Move your dreams into the real world before you invest in them.

25   Stop working

One of the goals that many of us have is actually a bit strange: we want to make a lot of money so we can do nothing. We have this desire when we hate our occupation, when we stop moving towards a career we'll enjoy, when we can't even believe we could achieve our financial goals through something we love doing. When we're grinding our noses at gruelling work, full-time loafing sounds great. Actually, it becomes miserably boring after only a few days.

Fortunately, the middle ground between hating your work and loafing all the time is the most fun of all: stop working and start enjoying how you earn money.

I haven't worked for years. Not that I've retired – few people have a heavier schedule than mine. I haven't worked for years because I love what I do. Let me give you my definition of work:

Work is anything you're doing when you'd rather be doing something else.

You can stop working too. There are just two steps to doing this, but both of them are big ones: (a) change your attitude, (b) guide your career into activities you love doing. The most gainful way you can be employed is at achieving the things you enjoy achieving. Why settle for less? You may make more money in the immediate future grunting along at work you hate. Over a longer time span your wealth and abilities will grow much faster doing work you love. Why is this true?

When you hate your work, you spend more time, money, and energy on pleasures. Less, perhaps nothing, is left for learning, growing, and striking out towards new goals. Unless we see work we hate as nothing more than a temporary stage on our journey toward doing what we love doing, we'll stay in this trap. We won't sacrifice to accumulate those precious few dollars of capital that our first move toward success will require.

If you suddenly learned that you were going to your first business meeting on the other side of the ocean two weeks from today, you'd start planning that trip right now, wouldn't you? You'd make flight and hotel reservations, arrange to have the necessary money with you, examine your wardrobe, renew your passport, and check on many other details.

26   Find yourself and then thrive through life-planning

Put a stop on work and a go on enthusiasm – pay the price to get an occupation you can love so that you'll be bringing happiness and success closer with every dollar you earn. If you spend your life doing something you hate, every day you punch in you're working at driving success and happiness further away.

Keep in mind that you'll never be able to find work you love until you become a positive thinker. Every job in the world is hated by some of the people doing it. By the way, after you've put lots of effort into changing your attitude, the first proof that you're succeeding will come when you start enjoying something in your present occupation for the first time.

You deserve a special reward when you achieve that breakthrough because changing your attitude is never easy. What it takes is three weeks of positive thinking. Put yourself on a completely positive mental diet for 21 days and you'll never want to go back to beating your prospects down with negativity. Three weeks of positive thinking and your life will never be the same.

Let's face it – some lines of work just aren't lovable. If there's no way you can improve your attitude enough to stop working and start enjoying your present occupation, change careers. If this is your situation, make the change with deliberate haste. Get moving. Time is precious and irreplaceable. But take enough time to prepare adequately so that your move has a solid chance to be up, not sideways or down. Success is not served by rushing into foreseeable setbacks.

SELF-INSTRUCTION:

'I don't work – but I do get paid a lot of money because I'm terrific at what I love doing.'

Most people will make careful plans for small trips and none at all for their longest trip, that is, for their entire life. Think about that. Isn't it amazing that more energy often goes into planning a vacation than organizing an entire career? Millions of people stick with their first job until it's time to look for a help-wanted sign again. They never plan their lives; they just react to emergencies.

Plan your life in writing. Review your plan monthly, or as often as necessary to make it a powerful force in shaping your success. Update your life plan at least once a year to keep it current with your growing horizons and changing interests.

Start now. Since the first page of the written plan for your life will be the hardest to write, quickly jot down something simple. To get yourself started, answer this question in writing: Where do you want to be five years from today? Then keep adding and changing details on your life plan throughout the rest of your days.

From now on, put a little time each month into refining and reviewing your life plan. That's right – never stop improving it. Especially when you retire, keep revising your life plan regularly. When your life isn't scheduled by work you love doing, take up the slack by scheduling non-work that you love doing.

Few things will give you a greater sense of purpose and importance than scheduling out your life. And few things will give you a greater appreciation of the pricelessness of time.

SELF-INSTRUCTIONS:

'I always get where I want to go because I preplan my hours, days, months, years, and my entire life.'

'My life plan is never finished because I'm always finding new ways to make my life better and new things to learn and enjoy.'

27   Put more months in each of your years

What skill or knowledge could you acquire that would help most to achieve the success you're seeking right now? Why aren't you learning it? Lack of time is a common reason. Think about what it would mean to have that skill or knowledge at your command. Then compose a self-instruction that will change your routine and save the necessary time from the hours that are slipping away from you now in trivial ways. A small amount of time saved every day can quickly make a large difference.

If you think that half an hour a day won't amount to much, figure it out. After taking Christmas off, 30 minutes a day totals up to 182 hours a year. Since the 40-hour week averages out at 173 working hours a month (163 if you allow for the usual vacation and holidays), this means that using an extra half-hour every day will give you more than a full month of added productive time each year. This is enough to make a big difference in accomplishing your goals.

A word of caution: start by converting just one half-hour a day from piddle time to goal-gaining time. After you've been on your new schedule for 21 days and are excited about the results you're achieving with it, think about adding another half-hour. Don't swamp yourself with a schedule that's too rough too soon.

The next time you wonder how someone gets so much done, you'll know – they have more months of productive time in their years than the average person has.

Let's take a quick look at an average midweek routine.

Getting ready	1 hour.
To and from work	1 hour.
Workday	8 hours.
Meals	2 hours.
Family, social	2 hours.
TV and other recreation	2 hours.
Sleep	8 hours.
	————
	24 hours.

On this schedule, how much time is left for pursuing your goals? Eight hours for sleeping? Come on. Teenagers need more. Sick people need more. And some adults really do need eight or more hours of sleep a night. But most of us don't need nearly that much.

Suppose that you organize yourself to feel great after only 7½ hours of sleep? Compared to the guy who slugs the bed 9 hours a night, this will give you *three* full months of extra time every year. How do you think the big winners win so much? Not by snoring longer. Put an extra month or three in your calendar by studying the fly-specks on the ceiling less. And you might find a few more bonus months in other parts of your present schedule.

SELF-INSTRUCTION:

'I always sleep efficiently and soundly, and get all the sleep I need in only — hours. Then I wake up feeling great, jump out of bed, and start making good things happen by using every minute of the day productively.'

28 Why cry about the cards you're dealt?

It won't change anything. Eighty per cent of the people don't care, and the other twenty per cent are glad. Don't give them the satisfaction.

Most people who lose at poker blame the cards. But, as any consistent winner knows, in the long run everybody gets the same cards. What makes the difference is how that standard run of cards is played.

It's the same in business and personal life. In the long view, everyone on the same track has about the same chance to find and exploit opportunities. Here are the basic rules for doing that successfully:

THINK AHEAD CLEARLY
No matter what today's business conditions are, they'll be quite different just a few months from now. Don't plan on today's fads,

trends, and economic realities continuing for long. They won't. Why am I so sure? Because they never have.

ACCUMULATE VENTURE CAPITAL

There never was an opportunity that couldn't be better exploited with money than without money. It doesn't necessarily take a lot – but it does take a little. Without that small amount of seed money, you're helpless, even when you're looking at a dazzling opportunity. Six months' living expenses is a reasonable minimum venture capital figure (exclusive of anticipated business expense) for the eager success-seeker to accumulate before a big move for independence.

IMPROVE YOUR CAPABILITY

While you wait for a favorable opportunity, push yourself hard to increase your knowledge, to improve your present skills, and to develop new ones. When you get your big chance, you will have less time – and the cost of making a preventable mistake will be much greater. So learn more now. Free or low cost night classes are available in most cities; and correspondence courses are available everywhere.

1. Increase your knowledge from the written word.
If you can't afford all the subscriptions you need to keep up in your areas of interest, schedule one evening a week at the public library and catch up on the latest magazines that cover your speciality.

2. Increase your knowledge from the spoken word.
Some libraries now have cassettes for loan on a variety of subjects. Buy those that will be especially helpful to you and listen to them over and over. The cassette's advantage is that you can learn while your hands are busy doing routine tasks. Go to all the seminars in your speciality that you can – there just isn't time enough to rediscover what's already known through your own trials and errors.

3. Increase your knowledge direct from the horse's mouth.
Many successful people will give you extremely valuable insights, information, and advice if you are respectful of their time and

show them that you're sincere and capable of becoming a success.

People who have recently retired from leadership in your field are especially good sources of instruction. A vital point: before you go for free advice, research the literature on the subject you want information on. There's no quicker way to turn the expert off than to ask the same old beginner's questions that are answered in every book and magazine article on the subject.

4. Increase your knowledge from your own experiences.

Do as much as you can. See as much as you can. Experience as many different activities as you can. Whenever possible, personally verify as much of the knowledge that you will rely on as you can. Experiences that you personally have and facts you personally gather will stick with you long after facts you've read or heard have vanished from your memory.

There's a danger here that leads many self-reliant and capable people into making mistakes. Although your personal experiences will give you insights and knowledge that you can gain in no other way, beware of them. Never forget that what you see or personally experience will have an enormously greater emotional effect on you than what you hear or read. But that doesn't, of itself, make what you've seen or felt any more important to wise decisions than other facts you didn't happen to see.

SELF-INSTRUCTIONS:

'I accept the cards that life deals me and then go out and win the biggest pots possible with them. Things I can't control never pull my attitude down because I'm always thinking about the great things I'm doing today, and the greater things I'm going to do tomorrow.'

29 P.R.E.P.P.I.E.S. don't fail – so be a P.R.E.P.P.I.E.

Why do some people win so much from life when others who seem to be just as deserving fail? Because **fail** is made up of Fear, Apathy, Indecision, and Lack of purpose.

Fear of small defeats makes us avoid small opportunities. When we avoid small opportunities, we don't have the chance to win small successes. Since every large success must be assembled out of many smaller successes, the price of avoiding all risk of small defeats is predetermined failure.

Apathy grips us when we realize that winning takes time and effort if we have been self-instructing ourselves that the only success we want is the instant kind.

Indecision robs us of our opportunities when we haven't prepared ourselves to make hard decisions.

Lack of purpose destroys our resolve when we have no worthy use for the things we want from success.

What about the 'preppie?'

Preppies have **P**urpose because they have a clear idea of what they'll do with the next stage of their lives after they've achieved the success they're seeking now.

They **R**espect themselves for their willingness to pay the price of achieving their purposes.

Preppies work **E**ffectively.

They **P**ersevere.

Preppies **P**repare.

They have **I**ntegrity.

Preppies put out **E**xtra effort.

To win the success you want, be a **P-R-E-P-P-I-E.**

SELF-INSTRUCTIONS:

'I want success in order to (insert your own purpose for wanting success).'

'I respect myself because I'm effective and because I persevere against rejections and obstacles that stop lesser people.'

'I prepare thoroughly for every important activity.'

'I have a high degree of personal integrity that leads me to put out extra effort.'

'I'm a preppie, and preppies are winners.'

30   Don't work for a down boss

If your boss won't recognize and reward superior performance, don't waste precious months of your life trying to change his or her attitude. The odds against that happening are tremendous.

Change jobs instead. Fast. You have enough negatives to cope with already. Don't put up with any you can get rid of this easily.

31   Train your subconscious mind for heavy problem solving

Examine the problem that you want to solve in detail. Define it as thoroughly as you can. Begin by writing the problem down. Don't skimp here. Writing out exactly what the problem is allows you to think effectively about it and begin reaching for a solution. To sharpen your understanding of the problem's dimensions, break it into parts. Then list those parts in the order of their importance. When you know exactly what the problem is and how it goes together, you're often at least halfway to finding its best solution.

When you don't want to write a problem down, this often means that you have fear mixed in with it. Since fear can be controlled or eliminated but not solved, its presence makes every practical problem harder – or impossible – to work with. Get the fear out of your way by putting everything down on two separate pages. On the first, list what's real and practical about the problem; on the second, list how you feel about it.

After you've separated the fear from the practical in this way, you can start moving on the only things that can be solved: the problem's practical aspects. The knowledge that you're working effectively on practical items makes it easier to separate intelligent caution from unreasonable fear. Then, when your subconscious mind gives you the solution to the practical problem, your fears about it will be eliminated.

List all the roots, branches, and leaves of the problem – don't forget to list the main tree trunk that connects them all. Find the limits, or set your own limits, on your problem. You can't solve any problem before you define it, which is another way of saying that you have to know a problem's limits before you can work effectively on it. When this is difficult, explore your needs more deeply. Get more information. Then sit down in a quiet place with nothing but a pencil and a pad of paper and write what you think about the problem. Split it up different ways. Outline all the possibilities. Then rewrite the probabilities in detail.

Remember that you aren't straining to solve the problem now. You'll let your subconscious do that in its own good time. What you're doing now is gaining a complete understanding of the problem. But the answer may pop into your mind at any moment.

This approach often gives surprising results: sometimes you'll discover that a worrisome problem has no practical aspects at all – it's pure worry all the way. Once you know that, you can take the bite out of the worry. How? By writing a self-instruction that will lay a positive new attitude over your old worry. That's step one. Step two is to review your new self-instruction three times a day.

Holding your thoughts on the reality of any problem is hard. If you find that it's easy, maybe you're merely letting stale old mental pictures flow through your consciousness rather than thinking realistically and effectively about the problem. Face all the facts you can identify; weigh all the evidence you can find; consider every possibility you can imagine; resolve every conflict you can pinpoint. Doing so forces you to learn many things and to make many small decisions. All this must be done before you can achieve the high state of knowledge about the problem needed to create a solution that will move your life upward.

Analyze the problem as thoroughly as you know how, but don't push yourself for the solution. What you are doing is loading the programme into your subconscious mind. When you have a clearly defined problem and all the information that it's practical for you to gather, the programme is loaded. Now cock the trigger of your subconscious mind by consciously thinking of how wonderful it will be when you have found the solution to that problem. After you've done all this, put it out of your conscious thoughts. If the problem comes back to nag at you, tell yourself, 'I've turned that one over to my subconscious mind. In due time, I'll have an

answer. But until then, I'm not going to worry about it anymore.'
Worry won't help you solve the problem. Your subconscious mind
responds to encouragement and confidence enormously better
than it does to worry and pressure, and it only works when it's
relaxed.

As you're lying in bed waiting for sleep to come, don't sweat and
groan about how deperately you need to find a way out – dwell
confidently on how pleased you'll be to have the problem solved.
Then drift off to sleep.

If the solution isn't in your mind the first morning after you put
this system to work, don't be discouraged. It usually takes several
attempts before you can master the art of allowing your subconscious mind to solve your problems. Maybe you didn't load the
programme into your head correctly. To guard against this possibility, reload the programme every third morning until you have a
solution. How do you reload your subconscious mind?

Restudy the problem. Go over every aspect of it. Review all
your suppositions, minor decisions, and information. Try to define
the problem a little more closely. Then spend a couple of minutes
thinking about how good you'll feel when you have this problem
solved.

If an exciting solution to the problem hasn't popped into your
head by the end of the first week, sit down for a moment in a quiet
corner and tell yourself that you know the solution will come to
you sometime, and that you're content to wait until it does. Then
do just that. However, any time you feel worried about that
problem, rethink it, reanalyze it, rewrite your written explanation
of exactly what the problem is and what form you want the
solution to take. As you do this, never recopy anything you've
previously written about the problem. This is vital. Writing fresh
and fast every time you reconsider the problem helps you break
through the barriers that are keeping the solution from finding its
way into your conscious mind. If you can't add anything new to
your thinking about the problem, don't let yourself worry about it.

Be sure to tell yourself, 'I really want an answer to this one. I
can do it – and I know I will.' Then relax. Put it out of your mind.
A week or more may pass. Then, suddenly, you'll have your
answer. It may be in your mind when you wake up. It may pop out
of nowhere as you take a shower, drive down the street, or wait for

an elevator. If the problem was an important one, your subconscious mind's solution will often astound you with its rightness and brilliance. Its answer will be the finest product of all your previous thought, learning, and experience; it will contain elements that you can trace to their source; it may point to new directions that will tax your courage and energy.

Once you've experienced this exhilaration, you'll start looking for larger worlds to conquer with your tremendous new power. Yes, it does take a little effort, concentration, time, patience, and self-confidence to bring it off. But what a thrill it is, what a vast source of confidence it is, to know that you have the whole awesome immensity of your subconscious mind at your command.

SELF-INSTRUCTION:

'I find my best solutions while I sleep. I do this by defining my problems on paper and then letting my subconscious mind take over. It always works because I have the patience and confidence to relax and let it work.'

32 Achievement's first demand

One of the most successful men I've ever spoken to isn't a captain of industry. He's not famous, not wealthy. When we met I was on my way to catch a plane out of Chicago after giving a seminar there. The airport limousine stopped at a toll booth on the expressway and a man stepped out of the booth.

The chauffeur gave him the money and the toll collector said, 'Thank you and have a wonderful day.' Then he bobbed his head inside the open window and spoke to me over the driver's shoulder. 'Sir, you there in the back, have a beautiful day.'

I glanced up from the notes I'd been working on, saw this man's huge smile, and automatically smiled back as the chauffeur put the limousine in gear. Then it hit me.

'Pull over,' I told the chauffeur. 'Something is wrong here.' I walked back to where the toll collector was standing inside his booth and said, 'I've got to ask you a question. Would you please come out here?'

He gave me a friendly look as he strolled out. 'What can I do for you?'

'How long have you been taking tolls?'

'Sir, this is my seventeenth year.'

'You've been standing in that box for *seven*teen years? Why are you so happy?'

'I'm only here seven hours a day. Then I'm home. I have a wonderful wife and wonderful children. We have this great little RV all fixed up the way we want it. Weekends – I've got enough seniority to get them all off – we jump in the old RV and go fishing, hiking, or just looking at what's on the other side of the hill. The pay and the pension on this job aren't bad, and our home will be paid for soon. I get all that just for standing here and taking people's money seven hours a day.' He grinned happily. 'I've got it made.'

'You really have,' I said. 'Thanks for answering my question.'

'My pleasure, sir,' he said, beaming on me.

I've never met anyone I could swear is happier and more successful than that toll collector. His work is necessary, he enjoys doing it, and he leads a beautifully balanced life. Whether he has it off or will be working, he looks forward to every day. His goals aren't challenging. But they are the goals he wants to realize, they are coming along right on schedule, and the future he wants is secure.

Many of us feel that success only means things like power, wealth, and fame. This is not true. Success covers a myriad of different purposes and accomplishments that people strive for every day. Many of the most lasting and satisfying forms of success, perhaps most of them, have nothing to do with acquiring power, wealth, or fame.

That toll collector is one of the fortunate few who are wise enough to understand and live by the most important requirement there is for success. This requirement, I'm convinced, is overlooked or ignored by more people than any other. We don't have to dig deep for the reason. Because it's so simple, only a fortunate few realize how profound and far-reaching are the decisions that must be made, carried out, and lived by in order to meet achievement's first demand. That demand is:

Before you can attain success, the effort you're making to get it has to be worthy of what you want.

33 Feather knowledge

Most of us have good instincts about feathers – we never pull a handful from anyone's tail unless we've decided that the pullee is a pigeon. People who deliberately mess with an eagle's tail feathers often move into smaller quarters – sometimes in the nearest hospital.

Most of us do know better. In childhood we all learn that we'd better confine our pecking to the easy ones. The trouble is, there can be a trace of the eagle in any cooing bird. Pluck one, and they may grow new feathers and turn into homing pigeons. You'll hardly ever discover the exact cause of your sudden new difficulties when a pigeon comes quietly home to roost – most pigeons are too smart to let you see whose beak is nipping at you unless you're way, way down. In that case, even the peck of a pigeon can feel like the rip of an eagle.

Other pigeons take the trouble to figure out exactly when an avalanche of trouble for the person who tweaked their tail can be set off by a flap of the wing or a little chirping in the right place.

Watch it when you're with the eagles but don't peck the pigeons either.

34 Burn the self-image of success into your brain

Your self-image controls everything you do. Since your actions and inactions are the largest influence on what happens to you, over a period of time your self-image not only controls everything you do, it also controls everything that happens to you. Luck, accidents, and the forces of nature and nations might seem to be totally beyond our control; in reality we always retain far more power to cope with how these events will affect us than we ever use. In the deepest sense, we create the results that those events have on us – by doing what our self-image tells us to do.

What is this self-image anyway? It is the design of your personality that you have created. You may have developed it carefully, or you may have done it carelessly – in any event, the personality you have is your own creation. It's no good saying that you are like you are because of an unsatisfactory upbringing or previous difficulties. The opportunities you didn't get don't count anymore. All these things are the unchangeable past – your life is the controllable present.

You will live that life in accordance with the chart of it that you've given your subconscious mind. Your self-image is the chart, the map, the blueprint of yourself – it's the layout of what you want from life. The greatest power that anyone or anything can have over us is our self-image. That power is so great that it would be terrifying except for one saving thing. Since we are the ones who developed our own self-image, we have the power to change it any time we choose to do so. When we do change it, our new self-image takes over and runs our life along the new lines we've set up. In other words, the self-image of yourself that you have created is the one that you will live up to – or down to.

We all have mental pictures of ourselves – it's impossible to function without a self-image. If you get a good mental picture of yourself as a winner, and an achiever, it doesn't matter what you look like physically. Please realize this. Some people think that successful individuals must have a certain look, a certain gait, a certain air about them, a certain way of talking.

They don't. All they must have is a self-image of success. Dr Maxwell Maltz proved this in his powerful work, 'Psycho-Cybernetics'. Dr Maltz was a plastic surgeon. He could help people who had burned, scarred faces, disfiguring birth defects, or facial features, a long nose possibly, that they were sensitive about. These people came to him and said, 'Change me.'

Dr Maltz would perform plastic surgery and transform each face into an attractive and often beautiful one. To his astonishment, he discovered that over eighty per cent of the people whose faces he had made more attractive were still as introverted, still as shy, still as unhappy as they had been before the operation.

After some years of puzzlement about this, Dr Maltz realized why. When only the outward physical appearance improves, the personality inside doesn't change until the self-image improves. In other words, nothing important changes until the self-image changes. If someone doesn't consciously start changing their self-image to fit a more attractive new appearance, their personality will remain exactly the same as it was before the cosmetic operation. Your self-image makes you worthy – or unworthy – of your ideals and successes.

Will you feel guilty when you become highly successful? Many people do. Let's see how it happens. After lots of hard work, you reach the point where you can achieve one of your most exciting goals, buying a new luxury automobile. You've had the exact model and colour picked out for a long time. At last you pick up the car and there's no way you can just quietly go back to work. You have to drive it around, show it off, share the news of your good fortune with others. So you tool over to see an old friend from your high school days.

'Look at my car. Finally got it. Isn't it gorgeous?'

'Must be a gas eater,' your friend says. He's just received a jolt. His opportunities, he knows, have been equal to yours – and now you've suddenly pulled far ahead of him. Unless he's pleased with his own self-image, the luxury car you've just bought is evidence both of your superiority and his inferiority. Your purchase of the car forced him to raise his image of you and lower his self-image. In comparison to you, he's falling behind – that's what your car means to him. If he has trouble with this, that's his problem. Don't let him push it on you by making you feel guilty. Part of the price of success is that the more successful you become, the less comfortable your unsuccessful old friends will be with you.

SELF-INSTRUCTIONS:

'I love success. I work smart and hard for what I get, so I deserve it all.'

'Nobody makes me feel guilty about being successful. If anybody can't handle my success, that's tough. I'll find new friends who can.'

You deserve your successes. If you didn't, you wouldn't have them. Convince yourself that you're worthy of the rewards that you earn. Guilt about success is unworthy of someone with your capabilities.

35 Where you'll learn

Did you pick this book up intending to learn how to be more successful and live a happier life? I hate to disappoint you, but you won't learn how from a book. You'll read how. You'll learn how when you take the ideas in this book, adapt them to your goals and strengths, and then apply them to your life.

We learn faster from a person who has shared some of our emotions and experiences. So let's make sure we have some things in common. Have you ever been depressed? Have you ever been frustrated with your life? Have you ever suffered guilt because you knew what you should do, but you couldn't motivate yourself to do it? Have you ever had too much month at the end of the money?

If you answered yes to any of those items, we have a lot in common. My goal in this book is to give you some ideas and techniques to help you live a happier and more productive life.

36 How to accept other people's anger

There are only three basic situations in which you'll face another person's anger directly:

1. You are in a stronger position than the angry person is. You're the boss, for example, and one of your employees is angry.

2. You and the angry person are approximately equal in strength. Your spouse, friend, customer, supplier, client, adult relative, or neighbour is angry.

3. The angry person is in a stronger position than you are. You're the employee, for example, and the angry person is your boss.

Simple enough, except that in each of the three basic situations your need to dispel the other person's anger may be great, moderate, or non-existent. You may believe that the other person's anger is highly justified, somewhat justified, or not justified at all. And the situation may be one that cannot now be changed.

One of the winner's most essential abilities is to be able to accept and resolve another person's anger when doing so is important to his success. To be able to cope with another's anger, winners know that they first have to control their own feelings. A winner sees another person's anger as merely another barrier to be overcome; a loser wants to use it as an excuse for losing control of himself.

If you automatically respond with anger when someone else gets angry at you, this means that anyone can seize control of your life simply by showing anger. Maintain control of your life by keeping tight control of your temper. Once you've done that, you're ready to cope with anyone's anger. Here's a simple and effective method for doing that:

1. Acknowledge the other person's anger quickly.
Nothing adds more fuel to a fire in someone's mind than having their anger ignored or laughed off. Listen to angry people. Pay close and obvious attention to them. Then tell them that you realize how angry they are.

2. Make it plain that you're concerned.
Say something like, 'I don't blame you for being upset – this is a very important matter. I want you to know that I take it very seriously.'

3. Don't hurry them.
Be patient. Let them get it all out. Never try to shut them up. Listen until they run down. In many cases this is all you can do, all you have to do.

4. Keep calm.
Many people express anger in such a general and emotional way that it's difficult to understand exactly what's bothering them. In this state, they're very likely to say things they don't really mean.

Let those things pass and take them up after you've solved the present problem – but only if doing so is absolutely necessary.

5. Ask questions.
Your aim is to discover the specific things that you can do to remove or correct the cause of the other person's anger. This often takes great patience. The angrier people get, the more likely they are to strike at the shadow instead of the substance of their anger.

5. Get them talking about solutions.
This is where you separate the reasonable people from those you can't help. If you've heard them out calmly, asked questions in a courteous and concerned manner, and are now exploring solutions, their anger should have cooled so that you can talk realistically with them. If they're still too angry to talk effectively about solutions, invent an excuse to postpone action and get back to them later. Let them do the rest of their fuming on their own time.

7. Agree on a solution.
After you know exactly what the problem is, you're in a position to look for some kind of action that will relieve the problem. Propose a specific solution. Start with the best you can do and tell them it is. This is not the time to get into a controversy over pennies.

8. Agree on a schedule.
When you've agreed on a solution, take up the schedule for it. Set up a realistic time frame that you're sure you can handle. Don't let the angry person push you into making promises you know you can't meet. You'll be tempted to do that, but the successful way is to meet today's problems today, not postpone them until they're larger tomorrow.

9. Meet your schedule.
Give this step top priority. You've talked your way into a second chance, so make sure that you don't muff it. If you do, you'll have an unsolvable problem with the angry person.

37   Turn grim contracts into happy agreements

Never talk about contracts with anyone. Don't even think about contracts.

Contracts are legal instruments. The word makes people think about the fees that lawyers charge, about legal complications and lawsuits, about all the fine print that they never seem to understand. To most people, contracts are bad news.

Talk about agreements. Think about agreements. Enter into negotiations with the intention of creating an agreement that will allow both parties to achieve their essential goals and to do what they both want to do.

Admittedly, this mood often fades quickly from an instalment sales agreement. The buyers receive all their benefits immediately and quickly get used to having them. From then on they tend to look at the agreement as nothing but another monthly payment.

The we're-both-getting-what-we-want mood is easier to keep alive in wisely negotiated agreements for joint ventures of all kinds. To achieve this long-lasting happy state, work hard before and during the negotiations to find everything you can that will help the other parties achieve their goals. Put as much energy into helping them as you do on spelling out your own position.

Why bother? Why help the other side? Because the best agreements are those that run smoothly from beginning to end. This only happens when the agreement does the most possible for both parties.

38   Don't break the law of unexpected consequences

Few of the major figures of history understood the laws of unexpected consequences. Napoleon's continued aggression taught his enemies the art of war and speeded the unification of Germany. Hitler's assault turned Russia into a world power. Russia's first Sputnik launched our space effort.

What causes a price war? Not oversupply. Oversupply merely creates the climate in which a price war can occur. Price wars don't start until somebody ignores the laws of unexpected consequences and tries to take business from competitors with price actions they can't ignore.

What are the two laws of unexpected consequences?

1. Every action in human affairs provokes a reaction of unknown force that is limited only by the power of those who choose to react.

2. Those who react will do so for their own reasons and in their own time. They will use their own methods and draw on knowledge and resources that are not entirely known to us. To the extent that this prevails in a given case, the consequences of our actions will be unexpected.

Before you make any important move, give careful thought to the consequences. There will be consequences, of that you can be certain. What's equally certain is that those consequences will come as a rude shock unless you look very closely into the emotions that your actions will cause your opponents to have.

39   How to get rich in five minutes

It's impossible to come up with a definition of *rich* that satisfies everyone. Fortunately, all we need decide is what the word signifies in our own scheme of things. Not many of us bother. We want to be rich without ever figuring out exactly what we mean by that concept. But undefined goals are unreachable. How can you expect to become rich if you haven't even decided what rich means to you?

Many of us think that a rich person is someone who lives as he chooses without having to work. Turley is in that happy position. Let me tell you about him.

Turley lives in an industrial district in the Sunbelt. Some years ago, he spotted a slab of concrete about the size of a two-car garage under an expressway bridge. The concrete slab was flat, dry and open on three sides. Turley saw its advantages right away. Plenty of shade. Cooling breezes. Hidden from view by landscaping. And there'd always be a dry spot on the slab no matter how hard it rained or where the wind blew from. Turley knew he'd found the home he was looking for. Over the years Turley added a few comforts – a discarded mattress, an old sofa, a few wooden boxes. Turley keeps it simple and plays it smart. No fires – a fire would bring the police. He doesn't need to lock anything up because he doesn't have anything worth stealing.

Every day thousands of cars crowd through the expressway below and hundreds pass over the bridge above, but they never see Turley come or go. When a man has a good thing going, he's careful. Turley doesn't mind the traffic's roar and exhaust fumes because he pays no rent.

About two miles away – easy walking distance for a man with Turley's leisure – is an industrial catering company. Their business is selling sandwiches and other snacks from lunch trucks to the employees of local factories. Twice a week they throw stale food away. On those nights Turley rummages through the trash bins and stocks up.

With food and housing taken care of so economically, Turley has no difficulty finding the time to scrounge what little else he needs from other trash cans. He gets up when he pleases. If the weather is bad he doesn't leave his home on the slab. But in good weather, which is most of the time, he spends his days in pleasant conversation with like-minded people. A few are always sitting around a friendly fire in one of the open fields nearby.

Turley lives as he chooses without working. Under the definition we started with, Turley is rich. You can do the same thing. Just reduce your wants until they match what you can obtain doing what you want to do with your life. Make that simple adjustment in your thinking and whap, you're there. No fooling – this is really what being rich is all about. Ask Turley if you don't believe me.

40   Understanding the nut

The necessity of cracking the nut every month can be a lift or a drag on your productivity. Getting through every month requires that you get your hands on a certain amount of money. The least amount of money that will keep unpleasant things from happening is your nut.

Some people – I'm one of them – work best with a big nut to crack. I relish the pressure. It makes me feel more vital, and spurs me on to greater achievement.

Everybody doesn't react this way. Lots of very effective people are pressure sensitive – very little of it makes them try so hard that they drive success away. Other pressure-sensitive people become so cautious that their productivity suffers. Instead of spurring these individuals on to greater achievements, money pressure destroys their confidence, shrivels their ingenuity, and exhausts them with sleepless nights.

Here's a success secret: discover what works best for you; then arrange your life so that you're working under that exact amount of money pressure. You'll have to learn what monthly nut will put that amount of pressure on you by experiment. When you're studying this question, don't give any weight to what you think should motivate you. The only thing that's important here is what actually does motivate you to higher production.

I've known salespeople who simply wouldn't work effectively unless they were about to have something foreclosed or repossessed. Then they'd suddenly switch on the hard work and become enormously creative and effective. Other people I've known lost all their flair for success under a surprisingly small amount of money pressure.

For most of us, the best-sized nut is one that we have to strain to crack, but it's not one that'll bend our bones. Then as we get stronger, as we gain in experience and skill, most of us need a larger nut to crack if we're to keep up our pace.

Know exactly what your nut is at all times. Review it every ninety days and decide whether its size is helping or hurting your march towards greater success. When you've made that decision, change your lifestyle to bring what you're committed to spend in line with what makes you earn the most.

If you work better under money pressure, leverage your investments and buy your rewards and luxuries on credit. Do this within reason, of course, and keep a wary eye on the general condition of the economy at all times.

If you perform best without money worries, never buy anything on credit. Rent until you can buy for cash; invest with cash only; buy luxuries with cash only. Above all, keep the nut you have to crack every month thin shelled.

41 Get your go-to-town money here

Millions of people stay in jobs they hate, or they settle for less than they should get, because they don't have any go-to-town money.

What is that? It's enough money to allow you to face change with a stout heart. How much go-to-town money do you need? Whatever it takes to make you feel strong enough to risk losing what you have now in order to reach for a greater opportunity. This is the executive's equivalent of a strike fund. It's the salesperson's ace in the hole. It's everybody's hold-out money.

Go-to-town money provides you with extra courage and clear-headedness to meet the surprises and alarms of life. If it improves your performance under the pressures of tough negotiations, it can double or triple your rate of climb. But if having go-to-town money makes you impossibly bullheaded, putting it aside will be one of the worst mistakes you'll ever make.

When they're involved in hard negotiations or any important decision, the only form of go-to-town money that helps some people is cash in the bank. Others gain confidence from money that's tied up in investments – equity in their home, for example.

In a moment, we'll talk about creating the go-to-town money you need from thin air. For many people, especially the success-oriented kind, this works as well as cash. The important thing is to quickly pull together enough go-to-town money of any kind to give you (a) the long view in decision making, and (b) extra courage in negotiations. Before you can start gaining the maximum benefits from your career and other opportunities, you must have enough.

Having enough go-to-town money allows you to pick the best long-term opportunity over less money sooner. You can't do that if you're being worried how you'll pay the rent, keep your car from being repossessed, and buy a hamburger for your honey.

Having enough go-to-town money allows you to display the fair degree of strength that it takes to win a fair shake at the negotiating table. A few people can make a convincing show of strength even if they're bankrupt. Most of us can't pull that off. We give ourselves away. Our financial weakness shows in many little ways – in our eyes, in our choice of words, in our tone of voice, and in our unconscious mannerisms. The person on the other side of the desk knows, often without knowing how he knows, that we'll settle for less. So he says, 'Take less or leave it,' and knows that we'll take it.

In thousands of negotiations every day, some people get less for just one reason: they don't have enough go-to-town money. Thousands of others get more for just one reason: they do have enough go-to-town money. Doesn't experience, talent, skill, and track record count? Yes – but the decisive factor in all negotiations is whether the individual has enough internal strength to convince the other party that he won't take less than what he should have. In most cases this boils down to whether that individual has enough go-to-town money. Courage is one part sheer guts and nine parts confidence. In a society that's organized around money, confidence is organized around money.

Never take money worries into a major negotiation. Worry weakens your resolve, clouds your mind, and does the other side's negotiating for them. Instead of cold-sweating about your money supply, discover the facts about it.

Work out a written budget. Let's say you decide you'd feel confident enough to bargain with strength if you had enough cash on hand to carry you for just one month. That's not much, but it may be the smallest amount that's realistic for you at this time.

Make your decision and then open a special savings account for this purpose. Even if the most rigid economies are necessary, build up one month's minimum budget in your special account as fast as you can. That money then becomes untouchable for any other purpose.

The exciting thing about go-to-town money is that all of it doesn't have to be real – most of it can be imaginary. If you understand how it's done, you can create enough go-to-town money in your head to give you a decisive edge in negotiations. You can't spend your imaginary go-to-town money – but you can sure use it to make real money with. How can you get your hands on some of the imaginary stuff?

Begin creating it by deciding how much you need. Ask yourself these questions: How long might I have to hold out? How much money would that take? What other income will I be getting during that time? How much can I cut my expenses without serious inconvenience?

Arrive at the sum of money you'll need to quiet your worries and give you confidence in any negotiation that you might have within the next year. Decide on how much of that amount you'll put aside in cash. The balance is how much imaginary go-to-town money you must create.

Do this by examining your other opportunities and resources. If you think in flexible and open-minded ways about all the legitimate opportunities that are available to you, you'll be able to list a number of fall-back positions. These are the kinds of work that you ordinarily wouldn't do – perhaps because you're over qualified for them. Nevertheless, in an emergency you can count on them for temporary income. For example, a line of work you're familiar with always has jobs available on short notice. The work is hard and boring but you can earn enough at it to meet seventy-five per cent of your minimum budget. Since you've saved up enough cash to meet one month's expenses, making enough to meet three-quarters of your expenses increases your hold-out period to four months.

In this way a few minutes of mental gymnastics was all it took to increase the effective amount of your go-to-town money by 300 per cent. List all the possibilities of this kind that you have and you can create all the go-to-town money you need, and do it a lot faster than you can save it. However, nothing beats hard cash in the savings account as a confidence builder, so don't rely on your imagination for every cent of your go-to-town money. If you try to do that, your resolve may melt in the middle of the first hot negotiation you get in.

The increase you're really looking for is in your negotiating confidence. Raising a large amount of imaginary go-to-town money certainly gives that to you. When the pressure is on, you can tell yourself, 'I don't have to take this – I can always work at —— until these people see it my way, or until one of my other opportunities comes through.' In other words, as part of your preparations for the negotiations, you mentally prepared a position you can fall back to, one that you can look on without fear. You did this so that you wouldn't be exposed to worry about the unknown in the midst of the negotiations.

So you politely turn down what they've offered and prepare to leave. What happens now depends on how the other person feels about three questions, and to ask them we're going to switch to the other person's viewpoint. (1) Do I have a solid economic reason for working with you? (2) Are your requirements reasonable? (3) From the emotional standpoint, do I want to meet your requests?

If all three answers are yes, the other party will always raise his offer.

SELF-INSTRUCTIONS:

'I have enough go-to-town money to hold my own in tough negotiations and keep my thinking straight on important decisions.'

'I have this tremendous booster for my confidence and performance because I never spend a nickel that I don't have to spend unless my savings account has $____ in it.'

42 How to make confidence create success

Unless you have confidence in yourself, you are forbidding others to have confidence in you. Everyone wants to hire, buy from, depend on, be friends with, invest in, and trust people who have confidence in themselves.

The reverse is just as true. No one wants to hire, buy from, depend on, be friends with, invest in, or trust anyone who lacks self confidence. They realize that everyone knows himself better than anyone else does. Since the world's best authority on the unconfident person has no faith in his ability and trustworthiness, why should they have any? This attitude is universal, so the first barrier to success that you must knock over is your lack of confidence in yourself.

How do you build self-confidence?

By making sure that you win often enough.

You do that by increasing your preparations and decreasing your challenge until they cross and you start winning regularly. When you find the level at which you can win frequently, hold yourself down to that level until you're convinced from scalp to sole that you're a winner. Once you feel that in your bones, start moving up. Prepare heavily for a slightly higher challenge, seek it out, and keep on winning.

You'll do all this best by coming up with an effective understanding of what winning and success are. It's not effective to run against a field of five hundred and believe passionately that you're a loser unless you come in first.

For some people, just being able to compete is in itself a splendid victory. Others have wonderful reasons for taking considerable pride in simply completing the race. In most contests, anyone in the top two-thirds has done very well, and being in the top half spells success in almost all areas of life. If you can make it into the top third anywhere, you're outstanding. Finishing in the top ten per cent is a tremendous achievement. Even the great ones don't win all the time.

Create an attitude towards winning that will build your self-image, not tear it down. Handle yourself like a wise manager does when bringing a promising fighter along – he makes sure that his fighter doesn't face anyone in his early bouts who could knock him out. Keep on challenging yourself, but stay out of the way of the punch you can't duck. Push yourself along no faster than your confidence and ability warrants.

SELF-INSTRUCTIONS:

'I win a lot because I overwhelm my challenges with preparation.'

Deliberately hold yourself back, and accept a lower level of challenge than you've set your goals on until you get impatient and feel strong enough to say this to yourself every day:

'I handle lots of losses and defeats without losing confidence because I *know* I'm a winner. Knowing that I'm a winner lets me risk rejections in situations that are impossible to completely prepare for. I'm strong enough to accept higher risks because I'm aiming higher.'

43   Anxiety anchors your action

I'm not talking here about situations where you're worried about an immediate and specific danger or problem. When you know what you're anxious about, you can throw all your energy into dealing with that immediate crisis. In such cases, it's healthy to feel anxious. When a great deal is at stake, a reasonable amount of anxiety brings out the best in you. What isn't healthy is to be anxious when there's nothing concrete to worry about.

Do you think that successful people have as much anxiety and stress as people who are not successful? There's only one difference between highly successful and average people – the highly successful use anxiety and stress to spur them on to achievement instead of allowing those feelings to depress them into failure. It's all in the way you look at the events in your life, all in the way you feel about them. Many men and women reach their most creative levels during periods of great anxiety. In situations where other people withdraw from the pain of stress, they bear down and perform prodigious feats.

How do you know when anxiety is grinding your competence down? If you have any of these symptoms, anxiety is attacking your effectiveness.

1. Vague feelings of apprehension.
Although there's nothing immediate and specific to worry about, you can't get rid of the feeling that a bad thing is about to happen, or that an uexpected good thing won't take place.

Sometimes this feeling arises because things have been too good. You forget how hard you've worked for the success you're enjoying and start to feel guilty about it. This happens to many new salespeople. Their huge load of enthusiasm gives them a terrific first three months. They don't know what they're doing. This means they don't know all the things they can't do – so they do well. That is, they do well as long as they keep on charging in there and throwing their fresh ideas against every blank wall they can find. Then, all of a sudden, they think, 'This is too good to be true.' Apprehension strikes. Fear makes them careful. They start playing it safe. And, pretty soon, that fear-induced caution brings them down to where they don't need to feel guilty – things aren't that good anymore.

2. Tight muscles.

Many times you can actually feel the tension in your muscles when you're in an anxiety-stress situation. Another giveaway is a sinking sensation in the stomach.

When the situation warrants it, there's nothing wrong with feeling anxiety and stress. Once you've learned how to cope with those feelings, you'll recognize them as helpers, not hurters.

3. Confusion.

When you start feeling confused, you're suffering from anxiety. You start asking yourself all sorts of difficult-to-answer questions. 'What should I do now? Go into management – hang around the office and keep an eye on the secretaries. Maybe I should, I've been in sales six months!'

All too many salespeople start to think like management, and guess what suddenly happens to their sales then? 'Well, I guess I should go into management, I can't sell anymore!'

4. Restlessness.

All of us are complex creatures. If you're restless and bored after moving ahead further and faster than you expected to, it's often a reflection of your anxiety about losing what you've so quickly won. And you have other problems – you're not as comfortable with your old friends as you used to be, and you haven't made yourself at home on your next level yet.

5. Difficulty making decisions.

It isn't the toughness of the problem that keeps you from making a decision, it's the stress. Stress that isn't handled properly, if it's high enough or goes on long enough, will make anyone timid. This effect can strike quickly. If you discover that you suddenly can't make a decision, you're suffering from stress.

6. Fatigue.

Stress tires you faster than running around a track. After a stressful day that included little physical activity, you'll be physically exhausted. But you don't get physically tired from enduring emotional and mental stress – you simply feel that way.

7. Difficulty communicating.

Ever wonder where your silver tongue went? If you suddenly don't know how to talk to people anymore, if all that remains is an uncanny ability to say the wrong thing, you're suffering from a bad case of stress.

All of these things mean that you're headed towards a mental depression. In the next section, I'll take up how you can turn back from depression and head resolutely towards a happier, more productive, and successful life.

44   How to avoid depression

The method is simple. And it's easy to put to work. The only difficulty is that we have to be willing to change our way of thinking a little. Here's how you can eliminate your anxieties and depression:

Read the following list of causes, and then change your thinking to eliminate any problems that you're creating for yourself.

Is that all?

That's it. You can avoid the issues and make your problems harder to solve if you wish. But if you want to get rid of your anxieties and depression, root out the cause and you'll start feeling great.

1. Disappointments.

When our investment in the thing we're not going to get isn't large, all of us can accept the bad news reasonably well. But after we've aimed at a goal for years and sacrificed for it all that time, the disappointment strikes hard and deep when we suddenly learn that it's not going to happen. This often takes place when people aim their lives at a goal for someone else to achieve. The reason for this is basic – someone else's goal is always beyond our reach because it isn't ours. You can have hopes and wishes for other people but not goals – their goals are something that only they can have.

I inflicted a disappointment of this kind on my father. When I quit college after ninety days, he went through a depression. All my life, Dad's burning desire was for me to become a famous attorney. My mom and dad saved enough to send me to college and I lasted three months. When I quit and came home, Dad was very depressed. He depressed me too.

But he gave me something then that has driven me ever since. My father said, 'Tommy, your mother and I have saved for fifteen years to send you to college. We'll always love you, even though you quit, even though you'll never amount to anything.' That was my first true motivational talk. That's the day the flame began burning.

Never try to live your life through someone else. Encourage your loved ones; sacrifice for them if you want to; but never forget that they are primarily responsible for their lives – and you are responsible for yours.

How do you handle major disappointments in your own life? First, fight as hard as you can to avoid the disappointment. If it comes anyway, set yourself down and shoulder the entire burden. Accept the loss. Make a list of all the things you'll miss because of that disappointment. Go over the list and wince once for every item. Then put a limit on how much more time you're going to waste mourning for what's not going to happen.

In other words, have a funeral for your disappointment. The disappointment was bad enough – getting depressed about it doubles your loss. Consciously grieve over your disappointment and put it behind you. Then go forward to the new things in your bright future.

2. Rejection.

There's a lot of it around. Someone you've given your heart to rejects you. Someone you've worked for years to help rejects you. Someone in whose hands you've put your entire life rejects you. Compared to personal rejection, business rejection is nothing. In sales training, I teach people not to take the rejection that's involved in sales work personally. The successful salesperson can have a door slammed in his or her face and go right on to the next door and knock on it. When you know it's not personal, rejection is easy to shrug off.

But when a loved one rejects you, or when a dear friend turns on you, you have to take that personally. That's when you say, 'What's the world coming to? That one hit me right in the gut. I'm depressed – I'm really depressed.'

Start using your head about healing your wounds right away. Begin by facing the rejection. Don't hide from it – accept it. You won't start to heal until you accept the rejection. Then let yourself grieve for a little while. Once you've let your grief out, push that rejection aside firmly and go on to new and more satisfying things.

3. Too much for too little.

Many of us set ourselves up for depression by avoiding reality when making plans. Costs are underestimated and income is overestimated. Unexpected expenses, taxes and inflation are not provided for. Our plans call for impossibly high returns on our effort or investment, and all facts that don't fit our dream are ignored. When reality strikes, it's devastating.

This will happen any time you allow yourself to get excited about the money you think you're going to make instead of getting excited about understanding and overcoming the difficulties that are involved.

4. Conflicting goals.

A lot of us eager people get caught up in this kind of conflict. When you decide, 'This month I'm going to spend more time with my family and I'm also going to work longer and harder than I ever have before,' what are you lining yourself up for?

A struggle with yourself. When your goals are in conflict, you have to lose the fight with yourself because all the effort you put into achieving one goal automatically drives you further from achieving another goal.

Get rid of the unnecessary anxiety that such conflicts cause by realigning your goals so that they complement and help each other instead of fighting each other. Unless you do this quickly, you'll lose confidence in the goal-setting system.

5. Sickness.

If you're not feeling well, it's easy to get depressed, especially if you've always been healthy. It's so important to take good care of yourself and keep your health. What's the point of achieving your financial goals at the cost of your health? Money without health isn't worth much. You can go into any large hospital and find men and women who've achieved tremendous things – but they didn't take care of themselves physically when they were younger. Today, they would give – and often are giving – every dime they've made to regain the health they used to have and threw away.

6. Unfair comparisons.

These can easily make you depressed if you build your expectations around other people's opportunities instead of around your own. 'Janie sure has it easy. The boss gives her all the breaks. Jack is wired in to the home office. And Jim is just plain lucky, no doubt about it – he falls into more great stuff in a week than I do in a year. They've all got it easier than me. Everybody except me is getting help.'

Rot. Put up or clam up. If you're convinced that you're unfairly treated where you are now, change jobs. Or accept that you're getting all the help and attention you're entitled to. If you want more, get busy and earn the additional help you want.

We can often recognize the six symptoms given above in ourselves. The next nine are easily recognized in others. If you care about someone with any of these symptoms, help them get out of the depression if you can. Unless you make progress within a month, try to get them into professional counselling. If you recognize these symptoms in yourself, the same time limit applies.

1. Loss of affection.

If someone who's close to you can't put their arms around you, if they can't say, 'I love you,' if they can't give you a kiss, if they've stopped sharing warm feelings with you, they're depressed and possibly getting close to hostility. Do you know anyone who's beating somebody up? The receiver is oppressed, the transmitter is depressed, and they both need help fast.

2. Habitual pessimism.

Depression is the normal state of the pessimistic person because they look at everything through the wrong end of the lens. They're always negative, always saying things like, 'It'll never work. It won't happen. It can't be done.' These people are depressed because they're pessimistic, and pessimistic because they're depressed. If something good does happen, they'll say, 'It can't last.' Then, without realizing it, they'll make sure that the good thing doesn't last. Pessimism and depression are two halves of a loop that can stay closed as long as the person lives.

3. Sudden loss of weight.

Emotional problems cause more people to have rapid weight losses than health problems do – if we accept the idea that there is any difference between the two.

4. Sudden concentration on trivialities.

People often turn to little things when they're too anxious to confront the big things in their lives. They get excessively neat; start collecting things; spend long hours gambling, gawking, or guzzling; they busy themselves with anything that'll keep them from thinking about their anxieties.

Escapism is a very useful and necessary form of relief – as long as it doesn't become the entree instead of the dessert.

5. Drugs.

Alcohol is a mood-changing drug, a more socially acceptable one than cocaine, of course, but it's still a mood-changing drug nonetheless. If someone close to you starts relying on alcohol or drugs to get them through the day, take action to help them.

Things will only get worse. The sooner you start doing something, the better your chances of success are.

6. Apathy

The apathetic have surrendered. Like Turley, they've decided that there's less pain in the trash bins of life than there is in the struggle for better things. This is the most serious symptom of anxiety of all because it means that the person has given up.

7. Compulsive eating or drinking.

Many depressed people stuff themselves because that's the only way they can have a celebration. Others drink their way out of depressions. In a down market stockbrokers are notorious for this. You think you've got problems? Let's talk about the sorry stockbroker when it's raining muck on Wall Street.

To be there when the exchange opens, Jack wakes up about three in the morning. The phone starts ringing as soon as he reaches his desk and the calls go like this: 'Jack, this is your closest friend. Why? Tell me why I lost everything.'

Another call: 'Jack, this is your mother. You told me it was a good stock.'

When Jack's long day comes to an end at 3:30 in the afternoon, he's thoroughly depressed. As he leaves his office, Jack says to himself, 'Soaking up a martini is the best thing I can possibly do right now.' He heads for the nearest bar and orders one. The next time Jack looks at his watch it's 4:15. 'No way am I fighting the traffic at this hour. Who needs more stress? Bring me another.'

Suddenly it's six o'clock and Jack realizes that he's missed dinner. More stress – now his wife is going to be mad at him too. Jack's only answer to this problem is 'Bring me another.' By eleven P.M. Jack isn't feeling the stress anymore. But it hasn't gone away. That stress is just waiting to climb back into Jack's conscious mind and begin all over again. It'll be right there with him when he wakes up in the morning.

8. Difficulty laughing.

When you meet a person who doesn't laugh, you've met someone who has a limited reserve of mental strength to carry them through life's repeated shocks. Laughter is the greatest and most natural treatment for anxiety in existence. Laughter doesn't give you a hangover. It doesn't magnify your problems. Your mental attitude is always better for having laughed at your situation.

You'll never have an ulcer while you're laughing. If you've stopped laughing much, start all over again. Finding things to laugh at every day is an art; the more you work at it, the better you'll get at laughing your troubles away – and the stronger your performances in every area of your life will be.

9. Difficulty sleeping.
People who have a positive attitude, get enough exercise, follow a sensible diet, and avoid caffeine rarely have trouble sleeping – unless they try to get too much sleep. Don't worry about insomnia – get rid of it. How? By changing whatever you're doing that's keeping you awake. Stress can build at night. Even a small amount of stress can grow into a serious problem over a long period of time if too great an intake of calories and chemicals is combined with too small an output of physical and mental effort. Many people don't sleep well simply because they don't demand enough of their minds and bodies – that is, they never tire themselves out. If your great goal is success, one of your smaller goals will be to usually go to bed happily tired out.

The whole key to defeating depression is action, not apathy. Find out what's getting you down; make the changes you have to make; then go on to the happiness and success that your positive attitude will certainly bring you.

45   Inoculate yourself with optimism

We all instinctively know that pessimism is more contagious than optimism. 'Laugh and the world laughs with you, cry and you cry alone,' is an old saying that's universally true. Most of the time we move away from the complaint and head for the smile because we'd rather be lighthearted, and also because we instinctively know how easily we can lose our glow of happy confidence.

Sometimes we can't get away from the pessimists, as when we're thrown in with them at work; sometimes we're unwilling to, as when a family member becomes depressed. Winners know that they'll often be in contact with pessimistic people throughout their lives. Do as the winners do: keep a tight roof over your optimism when it's raining pessimism.

People can be depressed for just a few days or they can remain depressed for the rest of their lives. When people you know turn pessimistic, be careful how you listen to them because your optimism won't make them optimistic. They are pessimistic for their reasons, so how can they become optimistic for your reasons? But, for reasons that haunt the dark places of everyone's mind, their pessimism can certainly make you pessimistic. This is why you can't afford to listen to the pessimists.

The natural world is more positive than negative: a little rain makes the desert burst with wildflowers; a short mountain storm soon gives way to long days of sunshine; life swiftly revives after every natural disaster. But in the urban world that we humans have created the opposite is true. Our traffic lights are red, yellow, and green – three colours – but we call them stoplights. Why not *go*lights? A weather report that it'll be partly cloudy tomorrow could just as easily be given as mostly *sunny* tomorrow. And why should we insist on saying colour-blind instead of grey-*seeing*?

Everything you say, think, and do gives you a boost towards optimism or a shove towards pessimism. When they're repeated thousands of times a week, even the smallest boosts or shoves add up to a powerful force in your life. And, very often, a single instance of thinking, speaking, or acting positively can give you a big boost towards success. It's well worth remembering that a single instance of thinking, speaking, or acting negatively can also give you a hard shove towards failure.

SELF-INSTRUCTIONS:

'I emphasize the positive in everything I do. I look at the good that can come out of every situation; I talk about the best qualities of every person I meet; I concentrate on the good aspects of every place and thing.'

'In both thought and speech, I choose positive words to describe everything I'm in favour of so that I will constantly be building my resistance to pessimism.'

'I say positive because success is positive and that's the side I always want to be on.'

46   You're entitled to have some fun with the pessimists

Handling the pessimism of others is a sanitation job. Avoid unnecessary exposure to the germs that pessimists carry, disinfect yourself after exposure to one of them, and make sure that you flush away their droppings.

If you're always exposed to the negative side of things, you can suddenly become a pessimistic person without even realizing what a profound change your thinking has gone through. Keep in mind that negative people don't know they're negative – they think they're realistic and that everybody else is messed up.

In my sales career I went through periods of intense activity, which meant that I would have an awful lot of problems and pressures to cope with. Going to the office some mornings, I knew that a pile of messages three inches thick was waiting for me, and I also knew that almost every message would be about a problem. Have you ever had a day when you wanted to drive right by the office and just keep going?

My fellow salespeople knew when I had a bad day coming because they had taken some of the messages. 'Has he got problems. Ho, ho, here he comes. Old Mr Positive is in trouble today.'

Before going inside, I'd have a little talk with myself. 'Hopkins, do not allow them to see you feeling down. Don't give them that satisfaction. This is the greatest day ever. Why is it the greatest? Because lots of people are trusting me to solve problems for them, and they have important money riding on my ability to cope with the pressure and get things done for them today. So I'm going to charge in there with a big smile plastered all over my face, and I'm going to give it all I've got – which is plenty.'

Then I'd walk into that office. They'd all be watching, all the negative folks. I'd throw that door open and call out, 'What a beautiful morning! Isn't it *great*?'

All the negative people would look at me like I had crawled out from under a rock, and what they were thinking would be written very plainly on their faces: 'I *hate* that guy!'

47 Keep your boat afloat

How do negative thought patterns affect your life? They give you the emotional droops. Your drooping emotions bring on a mental sag. Then your sagging mental powers cause a downturn in your job performance. That downturn leads directly to a sharp decline in your income. The decline in your income gives you more negative thought patterns, and they add more spin to your downward spiral.

While all this is going on, you've probably stopped exercising so that you can work longer and harder. That's a very popular reason for giving up exercise. But how many people who are in a state of mental sinkage actually use the time saved to work longer and harder? Most of them use the extra time to worry more.

We all go into declines. We all start sliding downhill now and then. Let me show you how to arrest your slide, get yourself turned around, and start climbing again. These are the general things you should be continuously doing to keep from getting exposed to depression.

1. Talk to positive people more.
Always be on the lookout for positive people. Actively seek them out. Encourage their friendship. Positive people are gems. Treasure every one you meet. Find ways to spend more time with them.

2. Talk to negative people less.
You can't do this passively. You can't just stand there and let anyone who comes along monopolize your ears with a flood of negativity. When someone is negative, you have to say to yourself,

'I can't help people like this until they're ready to be helped. In the meantime, I'm not going to let them hurt me. So I'm closing my ears to them – nicely if I can, roughly if that's the only way I can do it. My contribution to the world is enormously more important than hearing this pointless negativity.'

At times, this means that you'll be talking to nobody but yourself around the office. If that's the only way you can talk to someone who's up, so be it! Talking to yourself is always better than talking to a promoter of despair, depression and decline.

You might be thinking, 'Tom, I work all day with people who are negative. They sit at desks all around me. I can't get away from them.'

Yes, you can. You can get away from them in the only way that matters – mentally. If you're surrounded by negativity, put a positive shell around yourself. Let me tell you about the positive shell I used when I was in sales. I worked at it, of course – my positive shell didn't grow all by itself. But after a short time that shell was so thick that negative people very rarely tried to break through it.

Whenever somebody new joined the staff, I would greet them warmly and wish them well. Then I'd say, 'Now, I have enough problems to handle in my life already. If you have anything negative to say, don't come near my desk.' That got it out in the open right away. I wasn't there to win the Good Guy of The Year Award.

I stuck to my guns on this. Nobody was allowed to pull a chair up to my desk unless they were qualified to purchase. When anybody came over to kill some time, I'd reach in my drawer, take out a deposit receipt, and say, 'All right, let's see which one you want today.'

Do not let these people slurp you. In this life you're either a slurpee or a slurper. A slurper is someone who steals your warm emotions, absconds with your enthusiasm, swindles you out of your good feelings, and leaves nothing behind except bad news.

All you can ever really have in life is your enthusiasm and good feelings. Think about that and I believe you'll agree with me. You can have honours, awards, property, income – but all those things count for nothing if you don't have enthusiasm and good feelings about it all. How many famous and wealthy people can you think of who've committed suicide when they lost their enthusiasm for life? Don't give your enthusiasm and good feelings away to any angry loser who passes by. Keep them. They are the most precious things you own.

If you want to help Joe and Jane Negative, set a positive example. Be enthusiastic and successful. Laugh hard and work hard. Your example will radiate the message of positive-minded success to the lesser folk around you who are mired in moodiness and mediocrity.

3. Keep pumping.

Pessimism is bilgewater, and your life is like a ship. All ships leak a little, but that's no problem as long as the crew keeps pumping the bilgewater out.

Your pumps are your self-instructions. If your self-instructions are nothing more than the mixed bag that you've picked up as you go along, you'll be pumping a lot of bilgewater in, not out. Some people pump so much negative stuff into their lives that their ship sinks.

Think about what you're pumping into and out of your life with your constant thoughts that are negative or positive self-instructions according to your choice. If changes are called for, make them now. There'll never be a better time. Make those changes and start cruising happily towards the rising sun of success.

48 Begin every day right

Every morning, point yourself straight for a tremendously productive, happy, and effective day by starting out fast and peppy. Don't drag your fanny around for three hours. Almost every office has one sack of fertilizer who makes a big thing about how impossible it is to do anything right before noon. This is often the office wit, the ha-ha boy who knows all the ways it can't be done, the one who can put almost anyone's enthusiasm down.

I'll let you in on a little secret: Fred (or Fran) Fertilizer is morbidly afraid of the go-getter, the peppy get-it-done type. You can't be Fertilizer's friend unless you wear the same depressing sack, so don't even try.

Many people lose the next day before they ever get to bed because they don't get there soon and sober enough. Others lose it before they get out of bed by self-instructing themselves on how bad it's going to be. Another class of non-winners lose it by telling themselves that they always have to start slow.

How do you make a fast and enthusiastic start in the morning? Let me give you ten ways right now:

1. Listen to lively music.
Whatever you think is exciting, zingy, and upbeat will do wonders for your morning mood. Use cassette tapes, not the radio, so you don't hear bad news.

2. Listen to motivational tapes.
Alternate the music with good motivational tapes. I just happen to have made a few. I'd love you to start some of your mornings with me. And there are many other good motivational tapes.

3. Set it up the night before.
I believe in programming, so I decide the night before what I'm going to listen to the next morning to start my day. Whether I'm on the road giving seminars, as I am most of the year, or at home, I set a little stereo on the nightstand and load it before I go to bed.

4. Psyche yourself up with your own words.
After a coast-to-coast flight, I sometimes wake up with jet lag and a seminar to give. This means that I don't feel all that excited about getting up there and really pouring it on. First, I listen to the music or the tape I've selected. Then I say to myself, 'Okay, today is the most beautiful day you've ever had. Today you're going to meet the right people in the right place and time for the betterment of all. It's your obligation, Hopkins, to get moving because the people who are coming aren't responsible for how you feel. You must perform for them.'

Make your own motivational tape if this idea excites you. All you need is a cassette, a player-recorder, and some quiet time.

You can add to and smooth out your personal motivational tape in a few minutes any time you choose to.

5. Push positive thinking all the way.
You need it throughout all the areas of your business and personal life. This is vital. You can't be negative about large parts of your life and positive about others. Either enthusiasm will take over or negativism will.

— When you meet a customer, forget all your problems because your customer doesn't need them. You want to take care of those people because doing so is the career you've chosen for yourself. Always keep in mind that your chances of motivating people to do what you want are enormously greater if you're positive.

6. Keep positive books handy.
Have a good book, one that's positive and uplifting, on your bed stand at all times. Make a habit of reading some of it before you go to sleep every night. You'll find a list of the books I've drawn on through the years to develop my philosophy and winning business methods in the back of this one.

7. Stop putting yourself down.
There are enough people out there who'll do that for you, so don't you do it. We get started on putting ourselves down when we'd rather knock ourselves than hear the same knock from someone else. Then this habit grows. Pretty soon we're knocking ourselves for things no one else would think of. It's wonderful if you don't take yourself too seriously, but there's a wide difference between laughing at yourself over some little fiasco and knocking your abilities, courage, common sense, enthusiasm, and steadiness. You are the greatest person in the world. Believe that. Feel it deeply. You've got to love yourself first. Slow or fast suicide is the most sincere form of self-criticism known, and the reason people do it is that they've stopped loving themselves. Love yourself. You're the best person you know.

8. Build your family up.
It's so easy to fall into the habit of putting your spouse or children down. Millions of people do it excessively without even being

aware of it. Some spouses put their wife or husband down frequently, often many times every day. Many times it's a reaction that's aimed at keeping the other person under control. These putdowns damage a family in the same way that knocking bricks out of a wall damages a building. If this kind of destructive business is going on in your family, start the change to eliminate it by changing yourself.

9. Be generous with praise, stingy with putdowns.

Whether you realize it or not, most people who put others down do it to try to build themselves up. They often succeed – momentarily. But what they win with a putdown is an expensive and temporary victory. The person they've put down plans and plots until he pries open a weak point of theirs in order to get even.

10 Exercise.

Three workouts a week, every other day, is what it takes to keep your body fit enough so that your emotions and your body won't be a drag on your mind. Even people with physically-demanding jobs usually need a well-rounded exercise programme. Why? Because almost all workercise is repetitive: a few muscles and joints get all the exercise; the other parts of the body get very little. Funercise is different. Swimming, jogging, playing ball, walking – all these activities benefit the entire body.

Why aren't you exercising regularly now? Maybe your feelings about exercise were cut in a groove at school. Did your P.E. instructors make you do boring exercises over and over? Thousands of young people develop an enduring hatred for all forms of physical activity in physical education classes. What they learn there is physical de-education. Don't let a hangover from your school days keep you from enjoying your body and the pleasures of being fit.

Maybe you think you can't find the time for exercise. The truth is that you can't afford not to take the time. By eliminating the harmful effects of mental stress, a well-designed and regularly repeated exercise programme will improve the quality of your sleep and increase your alertness. It will vastly improve your attitude. It will help calm your fears, help keep your difficulties in perspective, and help keep depression away. By doing all these things, a regular and sensible exercise programme will raise the quality of your decisions and multiply your productivity.

Ease into your exercise programme slowly. Keep at it. Give it a high enough place in your schedule to get it done regularly, but don't become a fanatic. 'Okay, Hopkins, I'm jogging 18 miles a day now.' No. No. Keep your exercise goals and programmes balanced with the rest of your life.

During the first afternoon of my three-day seminars, I ask everyone to commit themselves to some type of physical exercise. On the second day of one seminar, a seventy-eight-year-old man bounced in and said, 'Tommy, I feel so good.'

'Why?'

'I started my exercise programme,' he said.

'What is it?'

'I'm committed to doing one pushup every morning.'

Will that one pushup really make him that much stronger physically? It's the mental discipline that's important. If that gentleman keeps at his one pushup for a while, he'll start doing more pushups; then he'll move on to increased physical activity of other kinds. All this physical activity will build more mental discipline and give him the base for yet more physical activity. Then he'll be on an upward spiral that'll work faster than the downward spiral of inactivity. Brain power and self-discipline grow out of physical activity. And what keeps it all going is self-instructing yourself that you love exercising and keeping in shape.

People who don't take care of their bodies – the ones who eat too much, drink too much, smoke too much, take too many pills, and exercise too little – start dying off in their thirties and forties. These people could enjoy life more, and do it for two or three times as long, if they'd take care of their bodies. We're talking big time here – thirty, forty, or fifty extra years of productive, happy life. It's a lot of time to eat up, smoke up, pill-pop, shoot up, and drink up in just five or ten years.

Your present body is the only one you're ever going to get. Think that fact through and start making some changes in your ways. Most mental health consultants are now doing everything they can to get their depressed patients on regular exercise programmes that will strengthen their bodies, put new power in their heart muscles, flush out tension, and increase their capacity to utilize oxygen. You don't have to pay one of those professionals to tell you to start exercising – you can start doing that on the floor beside your bed.

49   Making goals real

It's easy to achieve a goal. The toughest thing is to set realistic goals that you believe in and are inspired by, and then to monitor and update those goals frequently enough to keep them continuously powerful in your life.

It's amazing how many people drift away from the goal-setting technique after achieving some wonderful early results. Their first successes make them so busy that they stop growing. When that happens, they turn their backs on the most far-reaching technique for expanding their horizons and lifting their capabilities that humankind has ever devised.

To have goals that inspire you in the beginning, define them clearly. To have goals that are still inspiring in the middle of your drive for them, refine each one by adding exciting details as you learn more about them. To have goals that are inspiring all the way to the hour that you achieve them, take a moment every morning and night to vividly see yourself enjoying them.

Uninspiring goals are goals that you'll never stretch yourself to achieve. In other words, uninspiring goals are not strictly goals at all. To make your efforts pay back their full potential, keep your goals closely aligned with your latest thinking. That is, update your goals whenever you realize that you've taken another step towards a greater understanding of yourself.

You'll achieve many of your goals. Others you'll partially achieve. Still others you'll realize aren't worth paying the price for, given the new opportunities that have come your way. And you'll discover that some of your goals have moved into conflict with other goals that you've decided are more important. So you'll abandon many goals before achieving them. Never hesitate to throw out a goal when you realize it isn't what you really want anymore.

Difficult goals are achieved when you want them intensely

enough to make the fires of inspiration flame up inside you. Keep those fires burning. Review and raise your goals when the flames start to flicker – uninspiring goals are worse than worthless.

Defining and then refining and resetting your goals – and doing it all in ways that are inspiring without being unbelievable – that's where the work comes in. Anybody can achieve what they want. You can achieve anything you want to pay the price to achieve. But first, you must find out what that great achievement is going to be. The next step is to devise a series of exciting smaller goals that will lead you steadily closer to your great achievement.

50 Go for the largest returns

A trained seal gets a bit of fish after every little trick; dealers in casinos get paid after every shift. Hourly workers take a cheque home once a week; the same company's higher-earning salespeople take their commission cheques home once a month.

Real estate agents frequently wait three months for a transaction to settle and make their fee payable. Real estate developers frequently expect three years to pass before the profits from a new development are theirs to spend. Ageing their output so that it will command the highest price takes the producers of liquors and many other items even longer, and breaking into the highly paid levels of many professions takes at least ten years of training, experience, and all-out effort.

The world's most successful corporations are investing now in new products and processes that may be twenty years away from showing a profit. The world's most successful lumber companies routinely plant trees they expect to harvest after half a century has passed.

You may be considering a long-range project that involves investing time and money in a business venture or in career training. In either case, the project must be intelligently conceived and carefully managed throughout its term. New developments must be adjusted to and current expenses provided for. If all these requirements can be met, a wonderful thing happens:

The years that pass multiply the money invested and create dramatic profits.

If you want to realize greater gains, put yourself in a position to invest your time and money in projects that develop over a longer period of time. Why do the longer-range projects pay off so much better? Because there's so little competition. Very few people are financially capable of waiting, and even fewer are emotionally capable of doing so.

Twenty per cent aren't interested unless they can get it right now, and thirty per cent won't wait any longer than tonight. Forty per cent can't be bothered if the payoff is more than a week away, and sixty per cent never stick with anything unless it'll come through this month. Eighty per cent lose interest before the season ends, and ninety per cent are gone before the year is.

In other words, only ten people in a hundred are interested in anything they can't cash out of in a year. Of that ten, only one is emotionally capable of investing continuous effort and time in something that won't be profitable for five years or more.

The longer the time, the greater the payoff.

51   The art of regular feasting

Earnings come before productivity in the dictionary and nowhere else. In all endeavours aimed at making money, income follows action. Productivity leads, gain follows.

Getting busy can lead directly to serious trouble. It often happens after you've worked very hard and are starting to do well. You're putting lots of things in the payoff pipeline and feeling good. It's feast time every day and, because you're so very busy, you stop finding time for the things that made you successful in the first place.

Without realizing it, you're setting yourself up on a feast and famine cycle. Naturally, with your earnings headed steeply upward, you raise your lifestyle to meet your feast earnings. But, before the big payday comes, you've found places for all of your earnings that are in the pipeline. When the money finally oozes out and falls in your outstretched hands, none of it sticks. None of it gets added to your investment funds. It's already spent – already committed. A single session of bill-paying runs you back to zero again.

Then you suddenly realize that there's no more coming. Why not? Because you got so busy with current customers that you stopped making new contacts. Now you don't have anybody to put in the pipeline. You have to start all over and wait for the wheel to take a full turn before you'll see much money again. Meanwhile, you're running up bills. If you want to manufacture anxiety from the raw material of opportunity, this is the way to do it. It's surprising how easy it is for people to depress themselves by making more money.

If you'd rather manufacture success, a higher standard of living, and investment capital out of the raw material of your opportunities, look ahead. Set goals. Forecast your income at least six months in advance. Schedule, and then do, what you must do to meet your income goals.

This means that you'll block out a large part of every week and use it to keep a steady flow of new business coming regardless of how busy current business makes you feel. One more thing – keep the outgo that you commit yourself to below your current cash income or you'll never have a dime to invest.

SELF-INSTRUCTIONS:

'I never get so busy with today's business that I forget about tomorrow. I'm a planner. I look ahead. I'm always measuring my performance and eliminating unnecessary timewasters. And I always spend less than I make. When my tomorrows come, I'm always ready for them.'

52 Managing the basic resource

What is your basic resource? It's not money, not brains, not who you know. Your basic resource is time. Unless you use your time well, you'll never even get a glimpse of what your potential is.

Using your time well isn't easy – which is why so few people do it. We all have problems with organizing our lives, setting priorities, and planning our time.

Regardless of what you do in life, time is money. If I gave you a cheque for $86,400 and said, 'From this moment you have twenty-four hours to invest it. You can invest in anything you want to with this money. Whatever you don't invest, I get back tomorrow at this exact same moment.'

What would you do during the next twenty-four hours? You'd be out there working hard and fast to invest that $86,400, wouldn't you?

That being your attitude, why aren't you busily investing as much as you can of the 86,400 seconds given to you every day? That's right – at the beginning of every day we're all given 86,400 seconds. As each one ticks by, we've lost it forever in every way unless we find a way to invest that moment in the future.

The seconds of your life – and that's the way you live it, one second at a time – can be invested in countless ways that will bring you a future return. Many of those ways will give you repeated returns stretching over many years. You can invest your seconds in the creation of future income, in gaining new knowledge and acquiring useful skills, in making contacts, in enhancing your personal life. The methods of gaining future benefits from present time are myriad. And so are the ways of wasting time. The seconds you squander vanish forever. If you don't invest your daily treasure of 86,400 seconds wisely, in essence you hand them back at the end of each day to the force that gave them to you.

SELF-INSTRUCTIONS:

'I understand that life comes down to how I spend my seconds.'

'I don't squander my time, I invest it carefully and intelligently.'

'I'm always on the lookout for better ways to invest my time.'

'I maintain a strong defence against time-wasting people.'

53   Why time planning is worth more of your time

Most people don't set out to waste their time. They want something for it – in fact, all but a few of us want every nickel we can get for our time when we're selling it. This is as it should be. But most of us are less determined to wring all the other values from our time that are there for the taking. In other words, most of us don't work as effectively as we could at the business of becoming more productive.

The way to change this is through time planning. Let me give you some reasons why this is so important.

1. Time planning prevents future problems.
On some level of our minds, we know about most problems before they reach us. But usually we don't look at them until they get really severe. Why not? Because we haven't planned our time well enough to be out ahead of events where we can see clearly. Running with the pack, we can't see ahead, to the sides, or back. All we have time to think about is making our legs move fast enough to keep from being trampled by change. While we're doing that, unnoticed problems are growing. All of a sudden we're overwhelmed. Do you ever have days when there are so many things to do that you get nothing done?

2. Time planning banishes guilt.
One of the most common reasons for feeling guilty is knowing that you're not really working when you're at work. Putting your time in without being productive is deeply disturbing. Almost no one is comfortable with a tiny voice inside his head saying, 'What you do isn't worth a mudcake. You're a parasite, a bum. All you're doing in this world is taking up space.'

Unless your occupation involves keeping up with a production line, you have an almost constant opportunity to choose look-busy instead of get-it-done. In a wide variety of positions in both the public and private sectors, it's often very easy to act like you're working when you're not actually doing anything that's at all productive. When this happens society loses; your employer loses; but you lose more than anyone does. No one can win by trading their self-image as a producer and their commitment to excellence for the privilege of wasting time.

In all these jobs, you climb out of bed and get ready in the morning just like you were going to work effectively. You go to the office just like you were going to work effectively. You sit down at your desk just like you were going to work effectively. Then you can shuffle papers, talk on the phone, and confer with other people just like you were working and producing something of value. Are you really producing as much as you possibly can? If you're in any type of consulting or sales position, you can only produce when you're in front of someone who can say yes to your offering. Everything else you do is preparatory to that.

This means that in all such careers, anyone sitting in the office instead of being out meeting new people isn't working. In all people businesses, the ones who have the ability to meet more people every day are the ones who make the largest incomes. That's how they get more productivity out of their hours.

3. Time planning enhances your personal time.

There are two types of time that you can spend with your family – enhanced time and flop time. Setting demanding goals for yourself often means that there won't be as much time for your children and spouse as you'd like to spend with them.

What will you stop spending with them, flop time or enhanced time?

Let's define our terms. Enhanced time is time that's been planned with the family so that everyone gets as much pleasure and benefit from it as possible. This means that you go one-to-one with each person in your family to ask questions, and that you then act on their answers – that you truly share the decisions with your loved ones about how that time will be spent. Flop time is the time you spend with your family when you're too tired to do anything else. They know it's flop time – oh, how they know it. You're not doing your family or yourself any good by just flopping on them.

So pull your family closer together by cutting the flop time and giving them more enhanced time instead. What most people need to make this possible is a short exercise session daily – half an hour in a lap pool, a game of racquetball, a jog. Your work creates stress – what success-seeker's doesn't? Erase your mental tiredness and emotional exhaustion with a little physical activity every day, and then arrive home ready to enjoy some enhanced time with your family.

Some people will take potshots at you when they see that you're driving hard to achieve more than they have their sights set on. 'You're sure gone from the kids a lot. Probably don't care how they grow up, huh? Oh, yes, my husband could be more successful, but I want him home.'

I know men who are always home by 4:30. On Friday, they're usually home even earlier, and they don't leave until Monday morning. Many of their wives say, 'I wish he had the get-up-and-go to do something.' It's not that these men lack goals. We all know the type – some of my dear friends are firmly committed to three goals: (1) drinking a sixpack every evening, (2) never missing a football game on TV, (3) getting home from work by 4:30. Since they achieve these goals regularly and that makes them happy, this is what they should do. There's a vital point here: if you're making yourself happy, don't let someone else make you unhappy because your goals aren't like their goals.

4. Time planning creates self-discipline.
It literally creates a disciplined way of living. All of us have habits that are timewasters unless we've worked hard to eliminate them. Every business has a few timewasters; every relationship has some timewasting aspects. Here are some common timewasters that are gold mines of time that you can save.

a. Television.
Television is a wonderful invention. But like Kentucky bourbon, Swiss chocolate, or any other good product, TV has to be used properly. The problem today isn't only the time wasted, it's also the content. The average person under seventeen years old spends more time in front of the TV than at any other single activity. Be careful about that. Watch what people watch in your home.

b. Not doing it right the first time.
The next time you have to do something over because you didn't

get it right the first time, analyze how much time went into making that job right. Include all the discussion and hassle time that was involved. Keep track and see what percentage of things you're doing over. Then figure out how much extra time you'll save for productive work by eliminating rework.

Most people who analyze this realistically discover that rework is a tremendous timewaster. They find that doublechecking every task and job takes very little more time. A balance must be struck, of course. But it's safe to say that not many Americans are in danger of carrying perfectionism to an extreme today.

c. Not being organized.

Organize so that you can run your life. Unless you're organized, random happenings run you, you don't run them. People who get up in the morning with no plan for the day inevitably find that their day takes over and runs them in timewasting patterns.

d. Procrastination.

It's easy to avoid writing down what you should do. Most people don't want to make a plan for tomorrow because they know they wouldn't follow it. They just aren't that interested in doing what they know they should do. Every time they let their mind stray into thinking about what they should be doing, they feel guilty. So they close their minds to the simple, obvious methods that work. If they don't write down what they should do, they won't blame themselves so much for not doing it. You can play these little games with yourself if you want to, but the losses are still yours to suffer. Having and acting on a timeplan instead of procrastinating answers this question: Are you out to succeed or aren't you?

Look in the mirror every morning and ask yourself why you aren't the person you want to be. Stop blaming your family, stop blaming your company, stop blaming your friends, stop blaming the market, stop blaming the economy. Who does that leave?

e. Negative thinking.

All resentments and down-talk are brutal timewasters. Fear, anger, jealousy – they all lead you away from what's best for you. When you've tuned out whether other people are pulling ahead of you and what other people might be thinking, you can concentrate on the best thing that you can do with this minute. When you've reached the point where that's the main thing on your mind, you're solidly on the road to success.

SELF-INSTRUCTIONS:

'I make time to look ahead and see what's coming at me.'

'I feel good about myself because I always do the best thing possible with my opportunity time.'

'I use timeplanning to enhance the quality of my personal life.'

'I'm self-disciplined – I never let the boob tube rule my life.'

'I do it right the first time.'

'I'm organized because I plan my days and follow my plans.'

'I'm responsible for who I am.'

54 How to multiply time

Here are six powerful methods that I've used to save time and build an organization. They've worked for me, and they'll work for you no matter what you're doing.

1. Avoid flameout.
Understand that there are two entirely different kinds of time. The first is opportunity time, during which you achieve your career goals. The second is replenishment time, during which you rebuild your strength through exercise, recreation, relaxation, and sleep.

Flameouts happen to the people who never get the hang of switching from opportunity time to replenishment time. Unless you learn how, you'll run like a jet engine – until you run out of fuel. Then the flame goes out, your power shuts off, and you drop like a stone. Highly productive people by the tens of thousands suffer flameout, and they often lose several years as a result. Some quench their flames so thoroughly that they never manage to get their engines going again.

The dangerous part is that flameout sneaks up on you. Don't try to fly high when your tanks are low. Touch down and refuel your spirits – spend a few days away in a completely different atmosphere from your workaday world.

2. Get tough about opportunity time.

It's amazing how much of our working life gets eaten up by trivial interruptions unless we're determined not to let that happen. Successful people are tough about how their time is pre-empted by what other people think is important.

3. Get rid of easy work.

This is the usually pointless stuff that you like doing because it's easy, and doing it makes a marvellous excuse for not tackling the hard things you know you should do. If you're a winner, you always have time for the tough end of your job that produces the results – it's the easy stuff that you don't find time for. So find someone else to do these things if they really need doing.

4. Always jump on the most important thing first.

What is the most important thing that you should do right now? It's easy to figure out the answer – the most important thing is the item you least want to do. So jump on it. Get it out of the way. Then go on to the next thing you don't want to do and get rid of that item by completing it.

Start doing this every morning, keep on doing it, and you'll soon discover that you're not worrying anymore. You're enjoying the work, you're feeling good about yourself, and you know you're winning. If you want success, start your run at it by getting the least attractive and most important things about your job out of the way first every morning.

5. Touch it once.

This isn't a new idea. In some form or other it's an important part of every good system for digging out from under paperwork that

I've ever seen. If you'll take final action on every piece of paper that you touch on your desk, you'll be amazed at how quickly the mountain of paper choking your in-basket will melt away. Getting things done doesn't mean taking a whack at one thing after another and leaving them all undone. One thing completed is an accomplishment, ten things grunted at is a nothing.

Some people spend day after day rotating the papers from one side of their desk to the other. If anything, the heap of paper just gets larger and larger as new stuff comes in. Finally the day comes when it all gets thrown out, important things with useless trash. Then the party who just lost that paper battle (unless he's been replaced by someone more efficient) immediately starts building another great heap of paper. What does that heap of indecisions say to anyone coming near? 'Beware – somebody is working hard at doing nothing here.'

The way out is to say, 'This problem is going to get settled now. I'm returning that call right now. I'm finalizing everything I can; I'm getting my desk clear so that I can handle even more opportunities.'

6. Throw it away if you don't need it now.

One of the most efficient people I've ever known uses that saying as his motto. One day I was in his office and had a chance to observe his working methods closely. My friend keeps his desk clear at all times so that he can concentrate on just one item at a time, and he actually does throw a lot of things away that aren't needed at the moment.

But this man's definition of what he needs now includes keeping up an extensive and well-organized file of catalogues and other material that he can refer to quickly. Since he knows where he's going, he knows what he needs to keep. It all starts with a clearly defined set of goals, and that he has.

SELF-INSTRUCTIONS:

'I'm tough about my opportunity time. Nobody fritters it away. And I don't fritter my own opportunity time away doing easy work or engaging in unnecessary activities.'

'But I'm loose about my replenishment time. I really kick back and relax when I'm off.'

55   What's productive?

What's productive for you is based on your own personal goals. Are you with me on this? Lying on the beach in Hawaii and enjoying a two-week vacation is productive if you've earned it by doing the most productive thing possible with your opportunity time. It's productive for two reasons, replenishment and proof. You see, if you don't actually reward yourself for achieving production goals, you'll lose faith in yourself. And your family will lose faith in your motives for working so hard.

Is sitting around talking to people who are depressed productive? Not unless you've hung your shingle out and are getting paid for it. Many offices need a couch and a psychiatrist on duty at all times because everybody who's planted there wants to share their problems. Don't listen to your co-workers wail, groan, and mope – it'll destroy your enthusiasm if you do.

Working in almost any occupation means that you're in the business of solving a narrow range of someone's problems. Confine your problem-listening to that narrow range unless your productivity is directly tied to hearing about a wider range of their difficulties. Sales reps calling on the wholesale trade, for example, often become semi-pro psychiatrists. Since they're actually getting paid to hear problems, they're not amateurs. The rule is:

If it's not up, don't listen to it for free.

Over the years, I've seen that successful people – those who lead companies, build estates, and fulfil their potential – don't spend much more time working than many unsuccessful people do. The difference is that the successful have an ability to get more productivity out of each hour spent.

How do they do it? Their method is amazingly simple. In fact, it's too simple – very few believe it'll make any difference in their lives. So they never give it a thorough trial.

Some don't use the simple method because they lack a genuine commitment to paying the price of success. They are satisfied to spend their lives wishing for more without forming any intention of doing anything serious about getting it. They see success as something that's won by luck like a lottery prize.

If you see success as something that's earned, used the simple method. You'll find that it's enormously helpful, and that it will change your life profoundly.

The simple method is given in section 56, coming up next.

56   The simple method

How can you manage your time more effectively? I've given this idea to thousands of people, and many of them have written and said, 'Tom, it works.' Watch how simple this is.

1.   Focus on the six most important things.
Every evening, write down the six most important things that you can do the next day. Doesn't that sound simple? It is so simple that you'll have difficulty believing what an enormous effect doing this will have on your productivity.

Don't make it complicated. Grab your organizer, calendar, appointment book, or any piece of paper at all and say to yourself, 'Okay, I'm getting on this. Tomorrow the six most important things in my drive for success are ——' (Start writing them down.)

No. 1. _____

No. 2. _____

No. 3. _____

No. 4. _____

No. 5. _____

No. 6. _____

What does this exercise do? First of all, it's not an exercise, it's a system that'll work as well as you make it work. Secondly, it makes you think, and it focuses your mind on tomorrow before tomorrow is today and you're too busy coping with the moment to plan the day.

The simple method lets you build a dyke against the tide of trivia that has been flooding out all your hours. When you focus on the six most important things the night before, you're making tremendously important decisions about your future. You're taking command of that future. You may wonder, 'Is it really that simple to take command of my future?' Yes, it certainly is. Not very many people – fewer than one in a hundred – want success enough every night to plan their next tomorrow. You can put yourself in the top one per cent of all success-seekers by adopting this system today.

Jot down as many things to do as you can think of. Start by asking yourself, 'What should I have done yesterday that I didn't get done?' Then work on, 'What should I have done today that I didn't do?' Go on to, 'What are the most important things that I can do tomorrow?' Your first list may be impossibly long.

Don't let that bother you. Keep revising your first list until you have only six things on it. Use this system for three weeks and suddenly your mind will open up – you'll discover that you're finding items for your next day's list as you work, and at night you'll be able to think your opportunities and needs for tomorrow through quickly. You'll be talking to yourself along these lines: 'The North Arnew situation is coming to a head so I've got to get out there tomorrow. I want to see Smith, but our proposal isn't ready for him yet, so that's not a top priority for tomorrow. Carson is a priority item for tomorrow, but I can see Williams when I'm out that way next week. Oops; I've got to give Jones the bad news – all right, I'll call him first thing in the morning – unpleasant things always go to the top of the list.'

2. Rank the six items.
Rank the six items, not in the order that you want to do them, but from the hardest first down to the easiest last. If you'll be travelling to get the six things done, you'll route yourself in the most efficient order, of course.

When you have your six items ranked or routed, put tomorrow out of your mind until tomorrow morning comes. What you'll soon discover is that you will think far more clearly about organizing an efficient tomorrow when you're not faced with doing tomorrow's most important thing the very next moment.

Now you've taken the whole world of business and personal life and boiled it down to six things in order of priority. When you arrive at work the next morning, start on no. 1. If you're interrupted, take care of the interruption without getting involved in it more than necessary. Then, as soon as possible, get back to finishing no. 1. When you do, cross it out. Go on to no. 2 and repeat the process right down the list. Keep on that list of six until you complete it.

Resist being pulled off on to other things as strongly as is reasonable, given your job situation. Once you've followed this method for three weeks, you'll find that you have far more time that you've ever had before to cope with unexpected developments.

At the end of the day, you may have crossed only three things out. Some days, you may only cross one out. The vital factor is that you completed the most important single thing you could do that day. That one item puts you far ahead of the pack; lots of people *never* get their most important thing done.

If you'll tie into the six every day, you can't go wrong. How can you fail to find success very quickly if after a month you've done 30 things that were the most important items you could think of for each day? If you do six, that's 180 important items cleared. Continue that pace for a year and you will have accomplished 2,190 important things. By that time your entire life and viewpoint will have changed enormously.

3. Once every night.

Every night you make out a new list. Today's undone no. 2, no. 4 or whatever becomes tomorrow's no. 1. Your goal before you go to sleep every night is to have six things chosen that you must do the next day.

Just by deciding on and writing those six things down, you become better prepared to do them. Your mind will work on them while you sleep. Have you experienced this? As you lie in bed the night before an important business appointment, you're thinking,

'Tomorrow I've got to make this presentation. I'm going to show them____, and tell them____. Then they'll probably hit me with____, so I'll say____.' As you lie there in the dark the night before, the answers that pop into your mind may not be as convincing as you'd like them to be.

By the next morning when you're in front of that client, powerful words just flow out of your mouth. Have you ever been in this situation and said something so effective that it almost stopped you? You wondered where it came from.

It came from your subconscious mind, from a response your mind kicked out to the stimulus you gave it. You gave your mind the stimulus when you were lying in bed the night before mentally preparing yourself for the meeting.

But lying in bed might not be the best time and place for you to do your mental preparation. It works for some people; others prefer to prep their minds sitting by themselves in a quiet room. Experiment, then go with what works best for you.

4. It's too good to keep just for business.

There are two vital areas of your life. Write down the important things you should do tomorrow in both areas. Please start remembering the important things in your personal life. Your children's birthdays. They are so important. Your anniversary. Is that important! You can forget it one year and maybe it's okay, but year after year it comes off as though you want to block it out of your mind.

Write these things down. When you have personal items coming up, a friend's birthday that you want to do something about, for example, put it in your daily plan. When you're driving hard to succeed, it's so easy to let these things slide until you have no friends and no family. It happens to thousands of success-oriented people. They are like mirrors. One side reflects the brilliant image of their careers; the back is the dull grey of their private lives. Look closer and you'll see that the backing is corroding fast. You wonder how long their career-image will continue to shine.

If there's something your children want you to do three weeks from now, what does that tell you? It's important to them. 'Daddy, the big game is next month. You can come, can't you?' If you say yes, don't forget to write that game down on your list for that day.

It's amazing how many of us remember all the business things we have to do, but when it comes to something as critical as our children asking us to be there, we have a tendency to forget it. Kids can be put off. We take the easiest way out.

Children today can handle it when both parents have to work, or when you're gone a great deal striving to keep things going. But when they lay those dates on you two or three weeks in advance, chisel them in granite and don't let anything stand in the way of your being there. If you can't make the date because of a prior commitment, tell them right away instead of building them up for weeks.

5. Hang up your hang-loose image.
If you want more from life, achieve more. This means putting priorities on everything you do. Lots of people refuse to organize themselves because they have a hang-loose self-image. They're sold on following moods, not plans. Putting priorities on things sounds like self-regimentation. So they wander in to work each day and begin by checking around to see what's happening. Before long they're caught up in things that aren't really productive. Then all of a sudden the day is gone and some high-priority items have been neglected. After a month their production is falling behind; after a year it's only a faint shadow of what the priority-guided person has achieved. Whatever your self-image is, that's what you'll produce.

6. Commit to doing the six.
Commit to keeping your day going until you finish those six priority items. If you'll do that, tremendous things will start happening very quickly in your life.

Please put this book down right now and write out six priority items for tomorrow. Keep doing this for three weeks and, if you're sincere about becoming a success, you'll never go back to running your life like a street happening.

7. Give it twenty-one days.
All I ask is three weeks. Give me three weeks of every night deciding on and writing down the six most important things that you need to accomplish on those twenty-one tomorrows, and

watch how suddenly your life becomes organized. You'll be amazed to discover that you're completing up to three times as much as you ever finished before. It'll all come about because you'll renew your commitment to being organized every night. Twenty-one days is all I ask to prove this to you.

At my seminars there are always people who sit there and say, 'Sounds like a great idea.' Then they go home and forget all about it. Take a piece of paper now and get started. If you'll do that and keep at it, twenty-one days from now you'll have the most organized and productive life you've ever experienced. Your successful drive for the life you want can date from this moment.

57   Learning the knack of giving other people power

Unless you're willing to delegate, you can't create much. Everyone I've ever known who has built a highly successful operation has been quick to delegate. What have they given other people the power to do? Not just pesky details. These business-builders delegate large amounts of authority to deal with wide areas of responsibility.

Having other people do everything that you don't have to do is the best – and often the only – way that you can gain more time for the most productive and highest-paid work that you're capable of. As you grow, either you'll learn how to delegate more and more important things, or you'll quickly reach the level at which you are operating at capacity. Growth then stops because your time is fully occupied. In other words, beyond a certain point growth depends entirely on your ability to organize your work so that you can shift some of it to others. When you reach that limit, the choice is simple – delegate or stagnate.

This means giving up the easiest things about your job. The problem is, you may be telling yourself that you love doing those things. This is the point at which many highly capable people stop growing because they haven't updated their goals. They have reached a comfortable level that, although it's far below their present potential, it's also well above their recent expectations.

Why should they hire someone to do the easy parts of their work when they've met all their business goals?

If you've lost interest in career growth, you've lost sight of your purposes in life. When you stop growing you start dying. Go back to nature – get away to the wilderness for a few weeks. Renew yourself. When you've done that, you'll automatically take a clear new look at your personal and spiritual goals.

You'll come back with new goals burning in your mind. Start your move in new directions by concentrating your efforts on those few things that you can handle better than anyone else can because of your experience, skill, special talent, knowledge, and determination.

Focusing on those few things often takes mental discipline. To help you do that instead of piddling along on the easy work, keep your new goals and the money benefits of delegation firmly in mind. You'll have painful moments when you begin to delegate – your assistant will repeat lots of the mistakes that you haven't made in years. And, until your helper is trained, you'll probably lose time instead of gaining it.

But if you're delegating to get more done, not to build your ego; if you have a well-thought-out plan for shifting work to someone else; if you demand results, not mere compliance with petty rules; if you're willing to make working for you interesting and challenging – you'll discover that delegation pays large dividends.

58   Blueprint your life

In the daily scramble to make your best choices and then carry them out, a clear understanding of your priorities is a great help. You want to be sure that your heaviest efforts go into the best places. You want to get more done in less time. You want to maximize your performance. Then decide what your basic priorities are in a conscious and deliberate manner. Most people never do this – they allow their entire lives to be guided by the urges they were born with, and by whatever emotional priorities get clamped in their minds as a result of the things that happen to them as they go through life.

Such people often are motivated more by fear, anger, and revenge than by what will make their own lives better. Instead of concentrating on being more effective, they get involved in office cliques, political manœuvring, and score-settling. Their drive for success evaporates on this desert of negativity.

Want the best things for yourself. Know exactly what you want; know exactly how you're going to get everything you want. Know your priorities; know why you've set them up as you have. It's easy to lay out and follow the right daily schedule for yourself when you merely have to fit one day at a time into a fully thought out blueprint of your entire life.

Ideally, you would arrange your schedule every night and then follow that schedule smoothly through each following day. Realistically, you know that you'll often have to rearrange your schedule on the run. Every time you're forced to do that, you can't rethink your entire life-plan. With an underlying set of priorities, you don't need to – the most important thing to do next is always obvious.

As a success-seeker, what order of importance should you assign to the major elements of your life? This is a question that you must answer for yourself. My beliefs about the ideal order of importance follow. I hope that reading them will inspire you to make careful decisions about what your priorities should be at this stage of your life. Think these things through, make firm decisions, and then use those decisions to blueprint your life.

Many of us often think and talk about our obligations, our cares, our responsibilities – about all the things that we *have* to do. We're less inclined to think and talk about the things we *want* to do except when we're talking about leisure-time activities. One of the most powerful ways that positive thinking can help turn your life around is in this specific area. Let's take a giant step in this direction by revising our speech and thinking about priorities and privileges.

1. Family privileges.

All too often we think of the beautiful qualities of family life as obligations. Let's start giving our families credit for being the sources of the most worthwhile and lasting satisfactions of our lives. Your family privileges include the right to give your spouse and children the love and concern that only you can give. When you list the six most important things each day in the personal half of your life, think not of what you have to do, think of what you want to do. Head your list of family privileges, 'What I want to do today.'

Let's look at the ABCs of doing this right now:

A. 'Today I want to tell my spouse, "I love you."'
A good way is to just blurt it out. There are lots of other good ways – a small bunch of flowers, a mushy card, a treat of some kind. If you're one of those striving working people like I am, please realize that you've got to stop once in a while and say, 'What I want now, what I've got to have, is some closeness with my spouse.' Go off by yourselves, just the two of you, even if it's only for an hour or two. There's no greater compliment, no more sincere form of saying *I love you*, than wanting to be alone with someone.

B. 'Today I want to hug my kids.'
I love the bumper sticker that says, 'Have you hugged your kids today?' Show more affection in your family. If you're not comfortable showing affection, it may require a lot of talking to yourself before you and they get used to more closeness. The fact that your children crave your attention doesn't necessarily mean they'll welcome your first attempts. You may have to start slowly and train yourself by trial and error.

Keep at it. Children can fill up with rage they don't understand and can't express when they have been without the affection and concern that only a devoted and open-hearted parent can give them. If you haven't been that way in the past, don't be afraid to change; don't be afraid to grab your kids and just squeeze them. Let your warmth show; let your softness towards them come out. Do that and it will go far better than you think it will.

C. 'Today I want to whisper in their ear.'
Whisper what? How great they are. Nothing pumps more happiness and strength into a family than having praise and approval be a much more common event than criticism and punishment.

Any upward move of this kind begins when just one family

member starts relying more on the positive than on the negative. If this positive trend is continued long enough, patiently enough, and sincerely enough, it'll spread to the other family members.

What happens when a family gets even part way there? Everyone's self-image turns upward; everyone's happiness and performance increases; and success replaces failure as the most frequent happening in the family. The most talked-about things become what can be done and what wonderful things the world holds for us instead of what can't be done or what terrible things might happen. Certainly everyone will remain human; they will remain vulnerable to harsh words; they will still suffer disappointments and periods of decline.

But when the overall emotional climate in the family is one of support and praise rather than suspicion and criticism, the family's lifestyle will rapidly climb several levels, and then it will continue to soar even higher.

2. Greater cause privileges.

Here too, many of us think of obligations. But having a religion also confers enormous privileges. So does having a non-religious cause that we care deeply about. Let's stop thinking about our religious and cause obligations so much; let's start thinking about our privileges in these areas and about the many satisfactions that exercising them bring us.

You may not be a believer in an organized religion. That's your affair. But whether you've recognized it yet or not, you have a compelling need. That need is to serve some higher purpose with your life than merely gathering in as many dollars as you can. What is the point of it all?

The answer to that question should come before business. I know too many people who strive singlemindedly for the almighty dollar and completely forget the almighty reason that we have the ability to earn or possess anything. Don't lose that part of your life while you're achieving success. So many do. As they reach constantly for their monetary goals, they forget the joys and satisfactions and strengths that can only come from serving a higher purpose with part of their time and resources. The result is that their lives are outwardly successful and inwardly a shambles.

Don't let it happen to you.

3. Career privileges.
Whether you own the store or just work there, the business you're
now engaged in is today's bridge to your greater tomorrow. What
you're doing today is creating your future self – so treat today's
business seriously. Do the most productive work you possibly can
whether you're engaged in your life's work or doing a temporary
job. The additional responsibilities that you'll be given because
you're putting forth extra effort in a short-term step-up job will
speed and smooth your way for the rest of your life. It's never too
early to start building a confidence-inspiring track record.

Now let's take a closer look at your business priorities:

a. Past clients.
Too many people forget their old customers as soon as they collect
their earnings from serving them. Remember your past clients –
they'll give you or guide you towards future business. I used to
keep a file of the people who had let me serve them during the
previous year or two. Every day I would pull two or three cards
out of that file and contact those people to get referrals. Your list
of satisfied clients will give you all kinds of referrals, encouragement, new business, and information.

b. Current customers.
This is where tomorrow's income is coming from. These people
must get top service, of course. But while you're giving them top
service, you can't neglect a. and c. or you'll end up with z.i.p.

c. Future buyers, customers, clients, and projects.
Your current customers will provide tomorrow's income, but it's
your future customers who will pay your bills the day after
tomorrow. Schedule time for developing future business in order
to avoid the embarrassment and financial disaster of having to start
from scratch again.

4. Health privileges.
If it's threatened, your health immediately becomes priority
number one. When neglected, any of the lower priorities can
suddenly jump up to number one position, and they always seem
to do this at the most inconvenient times possible. The best

defence is to organize your life so that even your lowest priorities aren't ignored. When you've done this, emergencies rarely arise.

Health *privileges*? You better believe it. How smart is it to keep on telling yourself that everything about becoming and staying healthy is boring, exhausting, painful, and smells bad? If you're giving yourself negative self-instructions about keeping up your health, you're going to get negative results in things like how you feel, how much time you spend in hospitals, and how long you'll pay taxes.

The healthiest people enjoy physical activity, are sensible about what they put in their bodies, and give themselves very positive self-instructions about maintaining their health. Good health is the ultimate privilege; consider the alternative and then block out a large place in your yearly, monthly, and daily schedule for maintaining it.

5. Personal privileges.

Before the fires of ambition burst into flame in your head, you'll give first priority to personal privileges much too often. After that fire gets going, you'll have trouble finding a place anywhere on your schedule for friends, hobbies, and all forms of relaxation.

Busy people often neglect their close relationships and achieve success at the cost of losing those relationships. It's not easy to maintain them – maybe you simply can't. If so, don't feel guilty about it. Make a conscious decision and accept the disadvantages along with the advantages of that decision.

Many of your old friends won't go along with your career preoccupation. Don't be upset if some of them can't handle your success. It happens. Very few of your laid-back friends will want to understand your sudden need to achieve. When Friday night comes and you can't play cards all night because you have work to do the next day, some of them will say, 'Is business more important to you than we are?'

The best answer I ever had for that question was, 'No, it isn't, but I'm committed to do certain things.' Don't plan on explaining your work-commitment to their satisfaction because you can't – they don't want to see life your way.

Success has many prices. One of them is accepting the falling-away of your friendships with people who have negative emotions about your growth. When they realize that someone close to them is rising faster than they are, old friends are often jealous or resentful; they feel guilty that they haven't done as well.

It makes the friends you keep, the ones who are big enough to keep on liking you in spite of your success, all the more precious.

59   Success is the product of energy

After you've written down what you should do tomorrow, if it's like my schedule, you're going to need plenty of energy. A lot of people don't have the energy they should have because they don't know how to create and control energy.

Most of us think of personal energy as being of two kinds, mental and physical. Actually, there are four kinds of personal energy:

1. Mental.
This is the calculating power, the memory, the skills we've learned, and all our abilities to grasp and use new information.

2. Emotional.
This is the source of our fastest and most intense reactions and motivations.

3. Spiritual.
This is the fountain from which flows our deepest and most lasting purposes in life.

4. Physical.
This is the provider of all the other energies and the renewer of them.

There is an enormous difference between being tired in the head and tired in the body. We're all aware of this but very few of us order our lives around that knowledge. When we're mentally and emotionally tired, do we rest our brains and exercise our bodies? Not many of us do. Instead, we slump down in front of the tube and put more strain on our eyes, minds, and emotions. Our bodies are crying for exercise; our pent-up feelings are churning around trying to get out. But we plop down and bottle them up. Then we usually pound the cork in by eating and drinking too much.

The result is that our energy is not renewed. Sure, you'll get up the next morning and move through your usual work routine with your usual amount of energy. But will you get up charged with energy and itching to get at your opportunities? If you're a sincere seeker of success, you won't settle for less than the feeling that you're boiling over with energy.

The greatest source of mental energy is physical activity. If you're wise, you'll self-instruct yourself that you love it. Nothing else approaches the results that physical activity delivers in relieving mental fatigue and emotional stress. Nothing else creates more personal energy.

For centuries, many great minds have written of their convictions that most people have vastly more brainpower than they ever use. Within the last hundred years – and particularly within the last ten – solid evidence has been found that this is true. Helen E. Fisher reports that there are about 20 billion nerve cells in the average human brain, and that each of them is capable of transmitting electrical current to between one thousand and a hundred thousand other nearby nerve cells. Each of those transmissions between nerve cells represents a memory that can be recombined with other memories to create new ideas and capabilities.

Let's cut those figures in half and multiply 10 billion by 50 thousand – what do we get?

Here's what we get: a realization that the average person has such a huge amount of unused brainpower that any real understanding of our potential is totally beyond us. You and I are capable of being enormously more effective, original, and happy than we think we can be. The difference between our potential and our performance is staggering. Researchers into the functioning of the brain know that few people are using more than ten per cent of their brainpower, and that most of us are using less.

For example, a large percentage of people will tell you that they can't remember names, can't remember faces, can't remember jokes. Yet those same people remember the smallest details about

|

the things that really interest them for years without any difficulty. What explains this great difference in the performance of their memories? Just one thing, and it has nothing to do with how good their memory is. The difference lies entirely in the emotional intensity of their desire to remember.

'I'm using a lot more than ten per cent of my mental ability and physical energy,' I can hear you saying to yourself. 'I'm at least average, and I always come home from work exhausted because I've gone flat out all day long.' Sure you do. You exhausted yourself using the readily available ten per cent of your mental ability and physical energy. Like almost everyone else, you've never developed the rest of it.

You're only using ten per cent, so you have ninety per cent left. It's waiting in a reservoir that you can run a line to and start using whenever you choose to. It's yours – why not use it? How do you tap your untouched reservoir of physical energy and mental ability? By deliberately setting out to do so. Start by saying, 'Now I'm going to focus on creating more physical energy and mental ability.'

Many people think that the only way to succeed is to throw themselves totally into an all-out fight to climb higher. So they start putting in fantastically long hours every week, and at first they forge ahead rapidly. But the cost is high: the unremitting mental strain begins to sap their energy and health, and several kind of personal problems start to develop. An all-out drive can be carried on for a time – I did it for five years – but when you do this, you're risking serious trouble.

Within five years many hard-grinds discover that they're losing the cutting edge of their effectiveness. They feel themselves slowing down. No matter how hard they push, they just can't keep the pace up anymore. Now people they've been ahead of for years are passing them. What drives the hard-grinds crazy is that the passers seem to be doing it so easily. Now the ones forging ahead are the people who've been leading balanced lives. These are the ones who, although they've been working hard, have been doing it intelligently. They've spent less time working and more time keeping emotionally and physically fit than the hard-grinds have, so on the back stretch they're the winners.

The typical hard-grind learns nothing from this – his response is to try even harder. But more of the same only pushes his health, confidence, and performance back faster. Why are the hard-grinds beaten so often by the joggers, skiers, and tennis players? Because those physically fit people are far more alert. Because their range of interests is greater, they're more interesting to others; they know more; and they learn faster. They are enormously better at keeping things in perspective, which means that their decisions are better. And their minds are fresher from morning till night, because physically fit people have far more mental energy. They sleep better and have fewer aches, pains, illnesses, and emotional problems.

How do you develop more energy of all kinds? You start by putting your body in top physical condition. Unless you do that, all your other activities won't help much – you'll be stuck with the mental and emotional energy that you have now.

Most branches of the people business put heavy strains on our health. It starts with the way we eat. We get up, take a phone call at home, and we're running late. So we skip breakfast. Then we're late for our early afternoon appointment. So we skip relaxing at lunch. We grab a two-foot-long chili-dog belly-burner on the run instead. We have a late appointment. So we skip dinner. When we finally get home, we do the hundred-yard high hurdles to the refrigerator – and then we go to bed with the bowling ball in our stomach. Over a period of time, this is very tough on the body.

Take time to eat right and light. And take vitamins on a regular and reasonable schedule. Exercise on a regular and reasonable schedule. Your body will respond with amazing speed to regular and reasonable care. Give yourself three weeks of regular work-outs every other day. Start easy. You'll lose time, not gain it, by punishing your soft body with sudden hard exercise – all the advantages lie in training your body slowly, not in derailing it with injuries. If you get carried away and stiffen yourself up, don't count your recovery time in your six-week test period. That's right, six weeks is the trial period I ask you to give regular physical workouts. Don't make it drudgery – mix in all the fun you need to keep yourself at it. Everybody isn't ready for the jog pavement and pump iron routine that others love.

When there's any possibility that you might have a health problem, consult your doctor before you start on your exercise programme. The worst thing you can do is to crash on to a heavy programme of diet, exercise, and vitamin supplements. People who do this often drop the whole thing as abruptly as they started, which puts their systems through more vicious twists. Your body likes gradual changes. It's easily thrown out of phase or injured by sudden changes and violent strains it's not accustomed to. Learn how to treat your body as a friend and it'll show its gratitude.

Watch how much more energy you'll have beginning twenty-one days after you get on a sensible and regular schedule of diet, exercise, and rest. Within that time you'll feel great progress. Your body is a machine. Feed it only good fuel, run it through the right maintenance schedule, and it'll not only last much longer and look much better, you'll also enjoy it far more.

The great progress you'll feel within twenty-one days is just the beginning. Keep up your regular schedule of intelligent exercise and diet and within six weeks you'll know you're on to something great. Within ninety days you'll suddenly have a tremendous surge of energy. You'll find yourself working harder and thinking faster; you'll be more aggressive and less worried; you'll do more and sleep less because that's what you feel like doing.

You'll charge out to wrest the best from every day with more confidence than you've ever felt before. Your performances will be more polished and effective in both your personal and business lives. Your attitude will be so much better that people will comment that you don't seem like the same person. You've got the vitality – the charge – the feeling of sure success – that marks the winner.

From greater physical energy springs greater mental, emotional, and spiritual energy. If success is your goal, your first priority must be to pump up your physical energy.

SELF-INSTRUCTIONS:

'I'm on a consistent exercise programme (give your exact programme) and I feel great.'

'I love working out. A lot of people think it's boring. I feel sorry for those people because they don't know what they're missing.'

'I prize my exercise time because it lets me relax and get rid of the day's tension.'

'I have specific exercise goals. I exercise to build energy, improve my health, help me sleep better, and to prolong my life. I'm not out to stiffen myself up or tear myself down. So I move the pace up when I can, but I never do that faster than my body tells me it can handle.'

'I always eat and drink sensibly.'

'I'm working towards increasing my physical energy with regularity and good sense.'

'I take great care of my body.'

60 Putting your brainpower in high gear

Creativity comes from mental energy. Its foundation, as we discussed in the last section, is in physical energy. But developing your physical energy only goes so far towards increasing your mental output. How do you translate your greater physical energy into greater mental energy? Here's how:

1. Give up negative thinking.
It's not as easy as it might sound. Most of us are hooked on negative thinking to some degree. It's comforting. It excuses our failures. It allows us to avoid challenges. But when your mind is filled with negative thinking, your energy sources stop functioning. Your mind is goal oriented. When you are thinking negatively, your mind isn't working towards a goal. If it's not working towards a goal, what's the alternative? Suffering from fear, anxiety, and conflict or switching your brain off.

Success doesn't come to negative people. Negative thinkers have to turn their attitude around before they can turn their direction around and start heading for success. It all starts with saying, 'As of today, I give up negative thinking.' When a negative thought comes into your mind, stop it. Tell yourself, 'I'm not going to let that thought hang around. I'm not listening to that negativity. Out with it.' When you've cleared the weeds of negativity out of your mind, you're ready to plant the seeds of greater mental energy.

2. Set goals to work for.
The systems that work best for goal-setting are highly structured, not haphazard. Set goals for learning new skills, for income, for where you want to live, for your career, for the personal things you want to achieve, and for the things you want to do with and for your spouse and children. Nothing is more vital to your success than having your own goals clearly defined. Until you do, you're going to be pushed this way and that by everybody else's goals. We'll talk more about goals and goal-setting in the next several sections.

3. Work for achievement, not praise.
Many of us work for money only. I think that first you have to say, 'I'm going to work for achievement and accomplishment.' When you work for those two goals, guess what will just naturally come to you? Money.

I believe that money is the by-product of the accomplishments you reach. To most of the achievers I know, money is secondary to the satisfaction of accomplishment. This is a vital point. I talk to many people who are depressed in spite of having made large sums of money. A frequent cause of this depression is the conviction that they haven't accomplished anything worthwhile. Yet these people are thoroughly hooked on evaluating everything in terms of money. Even though making more money no longer brings them any real satisfaction, they can't shake that hook. Their needs for security and status have long since been met, so acquiring more money has ceased to be satisfying enough to justify the effort. Yet they can't think of any alternative that interests them. They have discovered that poverty in the spirit prevents the wealth in the pocket from putting happiness in the heart.

Their road out of depression is to cut themselves loose from a single-minded focus on moneymaking. This calls for widening their horizons to include other people. They have to renew their mental energy through accepting the challenges of a cause that's larger than they are. If you can say to yourself, 'I'm working for accomplishments and achievements,' you're halfway to the success that will give you lasting satisfaction.

4. Develop persistence.

If you're not a persistent person, you can become persistent. All it takes to get your first grip on persistence is twenty-one days of the right self-instructions. You can then gain a permanent grip on persistence simply by being persistent, and by occasionally repeating your self-instructions.

5. Demand more of your mind.

Stop saying to yourself, 'I can't remember names. I'm lousy at maths. I can't spell for sour apples.' You can do any of these things extremely well if you decide to do so. Let's take each of the above three common can't-do's and come up with specific solutions

a. 'I can't remember names.'
Dozens of books have been written on the subject of improving your memory. Many of them tell you how to remember Mr Bird's name. Mr Bird looks like a bird, you see, so you're supposed to put those two facts together. This is a good idea, but not everybody looks like a pelican or a rose bush.

Get to the heart of the matter. You know that, without any trouble, you would remember the name of someone who interested you romantically. How can someone whose memory for names is supposed to be terrible do that? Because you have an emotional reason to remember.

It's not practical to arouse romantic emotions about everyone you want to remember, but there are many other emotions that can be made to work just as effectively. Salespeople remember potential customers very well. Politicians remember more people because most people can vote. You can get emotionally interested in anyone you meet if there's a little time because everyone is a unique individual.

Here are the three major reasons why people remember names: (1) they focus their attention on the other person instead of being wrapped up in their own thoughts, (2) they find an emotional reason to want to remember the other person, (3) they catch the name when they first meet the new person, and then repeat that name two or three times within the first few minutes.

You can easily go a step further: at the first opportunity, jot that name down along with a line or two of description about someone you've just met. Include where and when you met and what their occupation is or what common ground you found. Put this information on 3 x 5 cards and review it weekly, taking time to recall each person's appearance as you see their name on the card. Do this for a few weeks and you'll soon have the reputation for having a terrific memory for names. You really will have – when you start telling yourself that you do.

b. 'I'm no good at maths.'
There are three reasons why you aren't: (1) you keep telling yourself that you aren't, (2) you avoid doing every bit of maths that you possibly can, (3) you never practise maths in private. Do the reverse of those three things and you'll become better than average at maths in a short time. Start by picking up a school textbook on maths to guide your private practice, and limit yourself to fifteen minutes a day of drill and study of the aspects of maths that bother you. Any good bookstore will have volumes that make the history and practice of maths exciting – don't cut yourself off from being comfortable in this basic area of success.

c. 'I can't spell.'
Of course you can't if you want to keep on telling the whole world that. Five minutes a day studying spelling will make a tremendous difference. Buy *Webster's Instant Word Guide* in any bookstore for the price of a chocolate malt – it'll make you a spelling whiz. Write down every word you have to look up on a 3 x 5 card and review it once a week.

What does it all boil down to? That you can be good at anything you want to be good at just by making an effort. Success-seekers aren't willing to be poor performers at any of the basic skills they need in their daily work and personal lives. And they know that beating average performance at any mental activity is a snap because most people spend all their time and energy telling themselves how incompetent they are instead of preparing to be competent.

SELF-INSTRUCTIONS:

'I never let a negative thought enter my head.'

'I always have clearly defined goals.'

'I'm driving hard for achievement and accomplishment, not just for money.'

'I'm the persistent type. Nobody but me can tell me *no* when I know I'm right. Then I'm the most persistent individual who ever pounded a sidewalk. But I don't beat my head against brick walls – my persistence is the smart kind. It's flexible. It's inventive. I find new ideas to bring to the problem, different directions to come at it from, other people to work through and give me help, and fresh inspirations to attack it with. When I lock on to something worthwhile, persistence is the game I win at.'

'I'm terrific at remembering names. I get a new person's name right in the beginning, I repeat it several times during my first conversation with them, and I make notes that I review occasionally to intensify my memory of that person.'

'I'm great at maths because I like it, I practise it, and I know a lot about it.'

'I'm a good speller because I understand how important using the language correctly is to my drive for success.'

'I'm amazingly good at (whatever you want to do well) because I've made the effort to be good at it.'

61 Teaching humour

It's often said that the sense of humour can't be taught. I agree. Humourless people don't laugh because they don't want to laugh. They've found something that's more important to them – spreading gloom and making sure that their predictions of disaster come true. This means that you can't change someone who is a pessimistic, humourless, depressed person into a cheerful chuckler just because *you* want to. *They* must want to move over to the sunny side of the street.

If you're the one who has the Ph.D. degree for being a Pessimistic humourless-Depressive, there's hope. You can change yourself by learning to laugh and enjoy living again anytime you decide to pay the price of laughing.

The price of laughing?

That's right. Everything in this world has its price. If you're going to bring laughter into your life, you have to give up whatever has been more important than being healthier, enjoying life more, and living longer. Part of the price of laughter is that you have to stop enjoying bad health. You have to give up your daily fix of bad news. You have to decide that looking at the bright side, not the dark side, is what you do. You have to start looking for the chuckle that's hidden in every situation. You have to start finding and enjoying the good that's in everybody. Then you have to give up the pleasures of grumpiness, of putting people down, of having ulcers.

Finding joy and success in the world is a matter of changing your self-image. You can do it if you choose to.

SELF-INSTRUCTIONS:

'I work hard, so I've earned the right to laugh at myself and the world. My activities are very important to me. In fact, they're so important that I wouldn't think of injuring my ability to move them forward by shutting off the healing powers of humour.'

'I always look on the bright side of things – it's just the way I am.'

'I know that laughter ranks next to sleep and food as a restorative, so I'm always on the lookout for an opportunity to laugh a little.'

'I have a great sense of humour, and it's getting better all the time. I love it when the joke is on me.'

'I always take a moment to sniff the roses, to glory in the sunset, and to see the funny side of life.'

62   Learn and use the techs that win

If the success you seek involves making lots of money, acquire a state-of-the-art *tech*nology. Then learn or devise some sophisticated *tech*niques to apply the technology with. You can't make much money in this fast-changing world with played-out methods.

But it will always be practical to make important money in old industries. Food is the world's oldest gainful activity, yet that's where Ray A. Kroc made his millions. When Ray walked into the original McDonald's a few years ago to sell food processing equipment, he immediately recognized what he was seeing. It wasn't some space age gadget to bounce signals off a satellite; what the original McDonald's had was the latest technology for making better hamburgers.

Kroc acquired that technology and proceeded to apply it with sophisticated techniques. In five years, the company he formed to buy one hamburger stand in California owned 3,700 stores throughout the nation and in other countries. Ray Kroc's personal net worth had run into nine figures. His secretary, to whom he had given a few shares of stock during the first year instead of the salary she was worth, retired as a multi-millionaire. From hamburgers. And all this happened at a time when America already had plenty of places to eat.

There will always be room at the top for everybody who has the determination to get there. An essential part of getting there is bound up in these two items:

(1) Find an effective technology and do what you have to do to acquire it.

(2) Develop your own advanced techniques to apply that technology with.

When you've done that, you're on your way to the top via the shortest route that anybody's ever found.

63 They're already obsolete

It isn't yesterday anymore.

It will never be yesterday again.

Yesterday's solutions were becoming out-dated by the time they were completely in effect.

Today they are obsolete.

We wake up every morning to a day that's at least a fourth gone. The world is changing at an incomprehensible speed, and that speed is accelerating all the time.

But the basic values don't change. We will remain our emotional, fault-ridden, imperfect selves; our amazing private inventiveness will still exist cheek by cheek with amazing stupidity; the astonishing complexities of our natures will not vanish – and events will continue to be decided by the collective mass of humankind's emotions.

Those who turn their minds around so that they only see the world through the eyes of the past are doomed to lose the present. Always look forward. Today's events are shaped by tomorrow's implications more than they are by yesterday's results.

What has been will never be again. Coping with that fact is life's more constant and basic opportunity. If you turn away from change, you turn away from life itself. Welcome change – it's what living is all about.

64   Create your own intelligence apparatus

In every field, knowing more sooner is the most common way of making more money sooner. The information you need comes in two varieties, public and private.

By public knowledge I don't just mean what's in the daily newspaper – public knowledge is the information that's made available to everyone working in a particular field. Many people aren't well enough organized to keep up with the new public knowledge that's constantly coming out in their specialities. What is the result?

They lose too often. The competitor who takes the business away from them usually doesn't have more professional ability – he just does his homework so that he knows what's happening in his field. Having and using good sources for the public information in your area of interest is vital to success. Attend conferences, seminars, and trade shows to help you stay abreast of new developments in your speciality; read newsletters, specialized magazines, and books; take training courses in the latest methods. If you're a beginner, get up early every morning and study until you charge past the average performers and catch up with the leaders. If you're a veteran, schedule time every week for keeping up, and for moving ahead of the pack.

Public information is very important to the success-seeker but private knowledge is even more so. Since fewer people have it, fewer people can act on it. So possessing private knowledge leads directly to moneymaking opportunities and is an essential ingredient in almost all financial successes. How can you gain this vital private knowledge?

In two ways, from others and from yourself. Develop your sources first. Your sources are individuals who have access to information that you can use. If you cultivate them, many people will give out an amazing amount of information for any of several reasons: (a) no one else pays much attention to them, (b) they have a grievance against the boss or the organization they work for, (c) they like you, (d) you can give them information they want in exchange, (e) they can't keep a secret, (f) they owe you one, (g) they have an axe of their own to grind, (h) you pay them for it in one way or another.

In most cases, you'll gain the most constant and reliable flow of information by trading what you know for what they know. This system works on trust, and things can't always be precisely equal: But over the long pull the value of the information you give must be about equal to what you get or that source will dry up on you.

Once you have a good flow of private information, you're in a position to move faster and more surely than most people can. If you have created private information through your own original – and secret – research, observation, and invention, so much the better. When you combine everything you've created with the information you've obtained from your private and public sources, you'll have a unique mass of data. The conclusions you develop by analyzing your unique data will be the most valuable knowledge that you can acquire. Unless someone else has followed an almost identical path, you will be the only person who has those conclusions – so all the benefits and profits that can be gained by exploiting them will be yours alone.

Your sole purpose in creating your own private intelligence apparatus must be to gather information that you can combine, analyze, and profit from, not to gather fuel for amusing gossip. Whenever you meet new people, be alert for anyone with useful information whom you can recruit. Sometimes all that's required to acquire a reliable source of valuable information is a pleasant little chat now and then with someone who is usually ignored.

65   When to jump ship

Hanging around too long is one of the most common mistakes of a serious nature that people make. The thing is, it's easier. The beer and ball game crowd is notorious for this; almost all of them will hang on to the bitter end with a sick industry or a dying trade instead of doing whatever is necessary to get into a rising occupation. They'll stick in the old job no matter how clear the signs get that it's not going to last.

For every clock puncher who will retrain himself and move to another state to take a new job, ten will sit around hoping the past will come back to life long after it's dead and buried. The majority of laid-off workers who have savings know what they should do, but they won't do it until their money is gone. Only then will they face up to their loss, dump the past, and move on to something young and growing that holds an exciting future for them.

When it's plain that your job is in jeopardy for causes beyond your control, don't wait. Act now and beat the crowd. Sell your house in the company town – you won't get much today, but you'll get nothing after the plant shuts down. Open up your mind to new lines of work. You need new job skills. Do what you have to do to get them. Make the hard choices now about the old and get on with the new.

When things are going well it's not as easy to recognize a jump-ship situation, and it's even harder to make an early move. But moving early is the surest way to maintain momentum. The common problem here is that people don't plan their moves; they stay with anything tolerable until they're forced to change. When is it time to jump off the ship you're on and catch another that's sailing in a different direction? Here are some thoughts to help you make this decision if you're an employee.

1. It's time to jump *before* you start aiming at any position that a relative of the management might want. In a company where somebody could marry the boss's daughter without having to resign, you won't get the job you deserve if a relative bright enough to breathe is eyeing it too.

2. It's time to jump when you realize that management is neglecting its basic business.

3. It's time to jump when your company has had a sensational run for several years. Since every trend plants the seeds of the next one, after several good years your employer almost automatically moves into the drop line. If you get out before that drop, you'll launch yourself off a winner. If you stay, you'll have to choose between stagnating and diving off a broken board.

4. It's time to jump when you have contributed importantly to the company's success but the arrangement you're working under excludes you from sharing importantly in that success.

5. It's time to jump when your job has lost its challenge because you've run out of interest and ideas.

6. It's time to jump when your company isn't keeping up with both domestic and foreign competition. If your entire industry isn't keeping up with foreign competition, get out of that industry. You can learn a new business quicker than an industry can revitalize itself.

7. It's time to jump any time you don't know why you're there. If your present job isn't part of a career plan, it's always a poor use of your time. Hang on to it just long enough to sketch out your career plan and find the job that will be your next step up.

66   Know the best time to sell out

Owners of small businesses are another group of notorious hangers-on. They start their businesses, work slavishly for years, and achieve a degree of success. Then they settle in to hang on until the end of time. All too often, they ride their business down far below the highest value it reaches during their ownership. When they eventually retire, they sell out for much less than they could have obtained many years previously.

Once you're successfully in it, the most important decision you can make about any business is when to get out. Here's when to take a close look at selling out and moving on to another challenge:

1. When it's going extremely well.
Your business may never look as good again. You'll be able to get a good bid from buyers for their rosy expectations of future profits when it's going extremely well. In ordinary times however, few small businesses sell for much more than book value – the buyers

pay about what the replacement cost of the inventory and equipment would be. Unless the business is very profitable, the labour and expenses that went into starting it up are thrown in for nothing.

2. When the long-term trends are down.
The most important trends to watch are those that apply specifically to your business, not those that apply to the overall national economy. If you see a bleak future ahead for your firm, don't wait until it arrives. Sell out now while it's relatively sunny.

3. When the excitement is gone.
Sometimes a business of your own turns into just another job that's emotionally not much different to you than punching someone else's time clock. If this happens and a good vacation doesn't change your feelings, set a time limit on how long you'll give yourself to rekindle some excitement. If that limit passes and you're still not keenly interested in your business, get out. You're not helping yourself or your operation by going through the motions of managing it after your emotional involvement has expired.

The next step after loss of interest is neglect. Businesses can survive change and mistakes, but rarely can they survive neglect.

67   Challenges and what to do about them

One of the best clues to whether someone understands the art of being successful is their reaction to the important challenges that come at them.

Those who will succeed have a characteristic way of reacting to great challenges, which may present themselves as opportunities, problems, or dangers. The succeeders set everything else aside when they believe that the right time to cope with a major challenge has arrived. Then they put all their energy into dealing with that challenge. They face it squarely, although this doesn't always mean they will make a frontal assault on it. Succeeders look at problems and opportunities realistically, but their solutions often involve slipping through the side door. They go with what works, knowing that frontal attacks are beaten off more often than they succeed.

Those who have chosen failure, disaster, and mediocrity do the opposite. They ignore the problem or opportunity as long and thoroughly as they can. Instead of facing the difficulty squarely when they finally can't ignore it any more, they moan and groan, run to and fro, and waste time trying to get help where no help will be forthcoming. Rather than taking action, they worry. When they finally make their move, they hit the danger with too little too late, or chase after an already lost opportunity in a futile effort to come from behind.

The key element in dealing with all challenges, whether they are problems or opportunities, is timing. When you're faced with a challenge, take fast and effective action that has a good chance of winning, or sit that one out. Make your decision early and then live with it. No move at all is better than a late move.

SELF-INSTRUCTIONS:

'I'm good at timing because I pay close attention to it.'

'I look on every problem as an opportunity to use my talent and initiative.'

'I see an opportunity in every challenge.'

'I move very fast when fast action is called for – but I'm also capable of calmly doing nothing when that's my best move.'

68   How to release trapped tension

If you're tense and uptight, it's because you have stress trapped inside you. Most people don't realize that this matter can be dealt with. Nor do they understand that it *must* be dealt with – the choice for all of us is between succeeding in spite of, or failing because of, tension.

You have three options when you start feeling the pressure:

1. *Keep your stress bottled up*.

Being civilized requires us to keep our tension bottled up much of the time. To a certain point doing that is called restraint and courtesy; beyond that point it's called frustration and ulcers. Tension is the garbage of your nervous system – if you aren't getting rid of it regularly in a positive way, you have garbage rotting in your system.

2. *Let your stress spill any way it will*.

The most primitive part of your mind knows that you have to get rid of excess tension and stress. If you fail to do that in a deliberate and controlled way, your subconscious mind will take over and get some temporary relief any way it can. Here are a few of the methods that your subconscious mind may use to spill its overload of tension when it's not getting any help from you:

> Illness.
> Apathy.
> Sudden outbursts of anger.
> Drinking too much.
> Overeating.
> Overuse of drugs.
> Talking too much.

Some distinguished medical researchers believe that most disease is triggered by mental stress, and all authorities agree that it is a key element in the development of health problems in many people. When tension spills into our bodies, it raises havoc. Usually only a little of the damage is immediately apparent.

Apathy is a common defence against tension. Since apathy almost always makes the ignored problems worse, it creates more stress. The usual result is that the person who is spilling part of his tension this way gets driven even deeper into apathy. Unless the pattern is broken, the apathetic person will sink until he reaches a level that's tolerable to him, a level that may be very, very low.

We've all known some usually calm people who are given to sudden rages. A few people have this way of getting rid of excess tension down so well that they make it work some of the time. But it often blows up in their faces because somebody has to accept their abuse. If that person turns on them, the resulting explosion creates far more tension than they were originally trying to get rid of.

Even from the angry person's viewpoint, this method of coping with excess tension doesn't make sense – abusing others gets rid of temporary stress at the cost of creating permanent enemies. When the abuse is physical, it's an even worse proposition because temporary frustrations then turn into somebody's permanent scars.

Drinking booze to get rid of tension is a cliché. Drinking an excessive amount of coffee or cola isn't so well recognized as an attempt to get rid of tension, but that's why many people do it. This is another method that doesn't work – caffeine and sugar intensify tension instead of reducing it.

Overeating doesn't work very well as a stress-reliever because it turns today's fleeting worry into tomorrow's stubborn bulge. It's like writing a bad cheque for something you don't really need – you get some immediate satisfaction at the cost of adding to your future difficulties.

Legal tranquillizing drugs are another ineffective method of coping with tension. The problem with tranquillizers is that the tension is still there under the chemical mask. Illegal drugs take today's temporary stresses and convert them into tomorrow's perpetual problems.

Talking too much does get rid of some tension. It also bores people, wastes time, and gives away secrets – which means that its effect on your future can range from mildly negative to deadly.

3. *Dispose of your stress according to plan.*
Schedule time for working off the harmful effects of tension; this will allow you to continue your drive for success without having to take long and costly detours. For best results, use all of the five methods that follow:

a. Laugh.
Laughing is the best and quickest way to lower the amount of tension that you're feeling. The only problem with laughing your tension away is that very few people have learned how to call some humour up every time they need it. If your stress level

is high, laughing won't eliminate enough of it unless you're a gifted comedian.

b. Sweat.

Sensible physical exercise has two great advantages: you can do it regardless of your mood, and it always reduces tension. When your regular routine includes exercise that's vigorous in view of your present physical condition, it will keep your tension level low enough at all times to allow you to absorb life's shocks with a minimum of stress.

Taking up an exercise that's highly competitive can put you behind the eight-ball of frustration again. So can any physical activity that demands a high degree of skill. Instead of reducing tension, competitive, skill-demanding sports create enough stress to largely offset the benefits of the exercise that's involved. But this depends entirely on your attitude towards the sport – if you can flail happily away and laugh off losing, you'll reduce stress. But if Boss Ego brings a must-win attitude to the games you're playing for mental relaxation, you'll lose the relaxation even if you win the game. The game means nothing – the relaxation means everything – but can you handle that? If not, stick to solitary sweating.

Many successful people use an exercise routine such as jogging to control tension; for additional conditioning and pleasure they play games such as racquetball. Whenever they feel stress building up, they jog longer and play fewer games until they feel loose and easy again. Nobody keeps score in the best exercises for relieving stress – swimming, jogging, pumping iron, aerobic dancing, punching the heavy bag.

A combination of both laughing and sweating is best. Put some distance between your problems and yourself by sweating most of your tension out. Then squeegee the last of it away by laughing with your friends.

c. Take direct action.

Some people sit around getting tense instead of taking direct action to attack the problem because they're too fearful, confused, or lazy to do what they know they should do. Others can't take action because the powers that be are holding them back.

Sometimes all it takes to relieve this kind of tension is to simply start doing something, anything, instead of just sitting there.

Inaction in the face of stress can be terribly frustrating – or very wise. If you know that doing nothing is your best move in a certain situation, exercise a little harder to keep your tension level down. Otherwise you might jump in from sheer frustration and make the worst move possible. When the winner is going to be the one who waits the other party out, set yourself up to win by waiting easy, not to lose because you can't handle your fidgety feelings.

d. Take *in*direct action.
Regret can cause an enormous amount of stress. You can't change the past, but you can replace regret with constructive action. When life hits you with a low blow, get extremely busy at your work. Do this and all of a sudden you'll discover that your problem and all the stress that went with it are forgotten. When things get you down, tell yourself, 'I'm going to work my way out of this thing. I'm going to get so busy that I won't have time to dwell on the past.'

e. Develop a love for action and doing.
I don't know if you have a love for action and doing. I think there's nothing more exciting than having a good action and a good doing and a good achieving. If you really love action, doing, and achieving, you're headed for the top.

SELF-INSTRUCTIONS:

'I always get busy when I have problems and work my way out of them.'

'I never overindulge to get rid of stress because I know that only makes things worse the next day.'

'I love action; I love doing things; I love achieving – and I do all three constantly, joyfully, and successfully.'

69   Tear off your labels

Don't let other people label you. Many people try to control you by doing this. They say things like:

'Oh, you're not going to like that.'
'Well, you wouldn't understand this.'
'Why aren't you good at those things?'
'It seems like you're not very smart.'
'I guess you better not try that.'
'You never succeed at anything.'

This happens to many young people quite early in life; their parents start giving them negative labels when they're still infants. Some parents keep on doing this job to their children even after they're adults because it's the only way they know: 'Honey, you don't have to work and strive so hard. Your father never amounted to anything, so – '

Don't accept other people's negative labels, and don't label yourself negatively either. The past is a bucket of ashes – throw them out instead of trying to reburn them. Wouldn't it be ridiculous to come home at night and say, 'I have some ashes; I think I'll start a fire in the fireplace.' Get rid of your ashes every morning – they're nothing but the past that you can't do anything about anymore.

A young man who has been a very aggressive, strong, and controlled person for many years once told me why he is that way. This young man vividly remembers the childhood incident that changed his life. He was small. His parents had told him not to play with a boy in his group who was known as a bully. But sometimes that isn't easy for a child to arrange, and one day the small boy was playing with his friends when the bully joined them. Before long, they were all jostling around. Then the bully lost his footing and it looked like the little boy had hit him. The bully fell down, hurt himself, and started to cry. When he finally got up, the only thing on his mind was getting away from the fierce little boy. So the bully ran home.

Somewhat amazed by this turn of events, that little boy said to himself, 'The way to get what I want is to be tough and hit first. From now on, I'm going to attack and be aggressive.' That incident burned indelibly into his mind. Today, the man who was that small boy is still aggressive, and he's still living by that label he put on himself so many years ago. He has completely thrown off the 'you're small, so you'd better run from trouble' label that his parents had given him.

Anything in your past that prevents you from moving forward and taking action today must be burned. Labels that are accepted and dwelt upon become believed. They become part of your self-image, part of the control mechanism that you use to steer your life. Have you ever had anybody say, 'I'm really not very lucky'? If they keep on saying that, what will they always be? Unlucky.

'I always have accidents,' is another common label people put on themselves. If you ever meet anybody who says this, make sure that you're never a passenger in a car he drives. (Even if you have to walk to avoid it, stay out of his car – a detour through the hospital never saves time.) People who say they always have accidents are telling the truth because they make it happen. Crazy as it sounds, accidents are what their subconscious minds think they want.

A good layman's understanding of a tremendously important area of our brain can be gained from Dr Joseph Murphy's book, 'The Power of the Subconscious Mind'. Dr Murphy shows that whatever you programme into your subconscious suddenly begins happening. The more you believe that something about yourself is true, the more often something very like that will occur.

People often say, 'Tom, it all sounds good, but I'm just not sure that it'll ever work.' When people say this to me, I refuse to be discouraged. I think positively for myself; I encourage others to think positively with every ounce of energy and understanding that I have – but I can't make a single person think positively who doesn't want to. So I tell doubters, 'You're right. If you don't believe it will, it won't.'

That's true of positive thinking, but it's really not true of negative thinking. Deliberate positive thinking won't work unless you believe it will and actually go ahead and use the techniques of positive thinking frequently.

But what about negative thinking? If you stop to analyze it, you'll realize that unless you're thinking positively, you're thinking negatively. Some of us like to believe that we don't think either positively or negatively, we just think realistically.

Are you like that? Do you say to yourself, 'None of this stuff applies to me because I don't think either positively or negatively. Other people do that; the only way most people can think is emotionally, but I'm not that way. I'm realistic. I see things as they are.'

If you really believe this, you are in deep trouble. Why? Because you're basing your decisions on a delusion, and that is always a risky thing to do. Nobody is emotion-free in their thinking unless they came from outer space.

Whether you accept the dynamic nature of self-instructions or not, every waking minute of every day you are giving a positive or a negative cast to your thoughts. That cast of thought then exerts an enormous influence on the decisions you make. Since what happens to you flows directly from your decisions, whether your thinking is positive or negative is the rudder that steers your life. The doubters can keep positive things from happening by refusing to think positively, but they can't prevent the alternative. Negative things will happen to your life in approximately the same degree as you indulge in negative thinking.

Here are some of the things we tell ourselves that cause us to make the negative decisions that lead to negative results. I hope you'll never say these four things again:

1. 'That's just me.'
Every time you say, 'That's just me,' you're driving one more spike in to make yourself stay exactly as you are.

2. 'I've always been that way.'
You haven't always been that way. You weren't that way when you were born. At some time since, you started telling yourself that that's the way you are. Start telling yourself that you're the opposite and very soon you will be.

3. 'I can't help it.'
You *can* help it. Decide that you don't do something anymore, keep repeating to yourself that you don't – and you won't. Rediscover the joys of doing what you know you should do – when you get the hang of this, nothing is more fun because the rewards are so great – and so constant.

4. 'That's my nature.'
If it's your nature today, it's because you've been telling yourself so. If you want a different nature, tell your subconscious mind what your new nature is. Drill it with creative and constructive things about the nature you want to be yours and that nature *will* be yours.

To make positive thinking work, remember that you have to phrase it in the here and now. Think, 'This is how I *am*,' about the way you want to be.

If you tell yourself, 'This is the way I'm *going* to be,' you won't change in that direction because 'going to be' isn't a self-instruction. Always think *am*, not *gonna*, when you deliberately self-instruct yourself. Why? Because that's what works. How can I prove this to you? Just think about how well what you've been telling yourself all these years has worked. You've just naturally been telling yourself *this is how I am* not *this is how I want to be* all your life, which is why you are the way you are right now.

SELF-INSTRUCTIONS:

'I'm lucky. Good things are always happening to me.'

'I never have accidents because I'm alert, use intelligent safeguards, and think ahead.'

'My nature is what I want it to be.'

70   Why some do and some don't

For years a question has bothered me. Coming from failure to a degree of financial success and then becoming a trainer, I have seen and personally experienced a wide range of conditions. I have been very low on money, achievement, and self-image, and have changed all that for the self-image and the actual substance of success. What constantly impresses me is how little difference there is between successful and unsuccessful people in intelligence and, very often, in how hard they work. Being a failure, or getting by only through long hours of labour, is not easier than being a roaring success – in fact, it's a whole lot harder.

The question that has troubled me from the beginning of my training career until recently is this: What is the essential difference between the all-around successes and the people who are all-around failures?

On one hand we see people who stay happy, healthy, and high on themselves; keep their humility; thank God for their blessings; and also achieve tremendous success in their lives. On the other hand we see people who can't manage to achieve any of these things. Exactly what causes that enormous difference between those two groups of people who have essentially the same mental equipment to begin with?

After many years of reflection on this point, I've finally come to the conclusion that it's entirely a matter of self-image. Those who succeed greatly have a great self-image; those who fail miserably have a miserable self-image. From this it's clear that in order to change a pattern of failure into a pattern of success, we must first change our self-image from miserable to great.

People succeed because they believe, not only that they can and will succeed, but also that success is worth the price they must pay for it. Believing that, they try harder, and this soon proves to them that determination creates growth. As they grow, the self-images that they are winners build in their minds; the sense that they are making an important contribution to the world grows within them; and they are no longer content to be a passenger on the highway of life – they must drive the biggest rig they can handle. Their talents, self-images, energies, and successes fall into a stable structure that spins powerfully throughout their active lives, generating enormous currents of productivity as it whirls.

That sort of self-image isn't created overnight. It's the product – the inevitable, certain, absolutely sure product – of the determination to pay the price of success. An inescapable part of that price is to accept the fact that success is a many-headed thing. A successful life cannot depend on the achievement of a single goal that other people can deny you.

If you make the decision to pay the price of many-headed success by forming a closed loop of greater effort and greater self-image, you will be successful.

SELF-INSTRUCTION:

'Success is worth far more than its price. I'm a driver in this world, not a passenger – I'm a shaker and doer. I love to go at it all out. Because I'm such a driver, I'm growing rapidly in knowledge, influence, power, and wealth.

71 Energy-draining factors

There are two ways to increase your energy: create more and lose less. We've already talked about creating more energy, now let's talk about plugging the leaks that are siphoning off much of your drive. Those leaks are much easier to control when you know about them. These are the things you need to guard against:

1. Confusion.
Confusion results when you're pitting one part of yourself against another part of yourself. Do you agree that the most difficult arguments we have are with ourselves? 'I should do this. I should do that. Maybe I shouldn't do this. Maybe I better do that.'

In many cases the best possible solution is to just do something. Then work on your priorities, goals, and purposes when you're at leisure.

Don't neglect this. How can you inspire yourself – how can you nerve yourself to do greater things than you've ever done before – how can you unlock the vast treasures of your potential unless you know exactly what all this effort will gain you. Every extra detail that you know about what you want increases your drive and decreases your confusion.

It also helps immensely to know a great deal about what you're supposed to be doing in your career and other investing activities. So dig in; hit the books; attend night classes; pump people's brains; think energetic thoughts; accept new challenges. In between doing that, get out and throw your guesses and eagerness against the world. The best way to find out what you don't know is to test what you think you do know.

2. Not being physically fit.
If you're not physically fit, I guarantee that someday most of your energy will suddenly start draining away. It may not happen today – it may not happen soon – but you can't ignore fitness forever without paying penalties.

3. Compulsive thoughts.
If you're troubled by fearful thoughts that you can't put out of your mind, write them down. Organize them carefully; that is, break them down into clearcut statements of exactly what is bothering you. Then set up a programme to deal with each problem. Most emotional thoughts can be dealt with by writing and reviewing a self-instruction stating that you are now comfortable about what used to bother you. Concrete problems will require concrete solutions.

Look at a big problem realistically. That is, see it as a series of small steps to a solution. Break the big problem into the smallest series of steps that you can imagine – then take on those steps one at a time.

If doing any of this is beyond you, or if trying to do it seems to make a problem worse, don't turn your back. See a professional and get help. Millions of people have benefitted enormously from therapy at the right time.

4. Alcohol and other mind-changing drugs.
These ventures into chemically-induced unreality exact a heavy

price. If you get hooked on anything except the natural way of living, that price can be your life.

5. Fear of failing.
We're all afraid to fail, but failure is part of life. It's the way we learn. Overcome the fear of failing by doing what you fear most. After you've done it, you'll forget the fear.

6. Self-criticism and guilt.
Don't slam yourself with 'What did I do wrong' accusations. Instead, build yourself up with 'What did I do right' praise. Then tell yourself, 'I'm consistently going to do that again and again and again until I'm turning in a superior performance.' Many new things that you start doing go wrong at first. If you compound your early trial-and-errors with loads of regrets and negative thoughts, you'll get slower and slower about trying anything new. Turning away from new things will be fatal to your plans – successful people succeed because they attempt more and regret less.

7. Worrying about other people's opinions.
You've probably got more good ideas than most people have, so don't worry about other people's opinions. Have faith in your own ideas.

SELF-INSTRUCTIONS:

1. 'I know where I'm going because I've taken the time and trouble to make that decision.'

2. 'I keep myself in top shape.'

3. '——— doesn't bother me anymore.'

4. 'I don't do stupid things like letting drugs control my mind.'

5. 'I'm not afraid to fail because that's how I learn.'

6. 'When I fail I look at what I did right, not at what I did wrong.'

7. 'I respect and listen to other people's opinions, but I have faith in my own opinions and make up my own mind.'

72   The three basic steps to wealth

People often ask me, 'Tom, do you have any ideas on becoming wealthy?' Will Rogers gave the best answer to this question that I've ever heard. 'Live on half of what you make and invest the rest in land,' he told his Hollywood friends in the late twenties and early thirties. Everybody who acted on that advice became wealthy. Many other movie people making big money at that time spent it all as fast as they could – and a few years later were dependent on handouts.

Today, living on half their income is not in the cards for most families, and making a profit on land ownership now requires far more expertise than it did fifty years ago. But Will Rogers' advice is still excellent for people with high earnings. In other circumstances, my advice is to follow this three-step formula:

1. Make more than you're spending now.
2. Every time you increase your earnings, increase the percentage between what you make and what you spend.
3. Invest your percentage in equity positions that (a) offer tax shelter, (b) take advantage of inflation.

Most people never get past step one whether their incomes go steadily up over the years or bounce down from time to time. The problem is that you discover powerful pressures and urges to spend more when you start earning more. Parkinson put it very succinctly: 'Expenses rise to meet income.'

My system for getting wealthy is only three short sentences and three simple ideas. Only a very few follow a system like this, and these are the people who acquire and hold on to a substantial amount of money. Those three sentences can give people at age sixty-five more than they'll ever get from the government or from a company pension.

All my system calls for is enough self-discipline to make more than you're spending so that you can accumulate capital. Additional income that's all immediately spent does very little for you.

What gives extra income enormous value is the fact that when it's wisely invested it will last your entire life. No one ever became wealthy without spending less than they made. If you doubt the importance of this, read the story of John D. Rockefeller's early days. Without the early savings he accumulated, the enormous Rockefeller fortune would never have been acquired.

Let me say it again: make more than you spend, then keep on spending less than you've made. This calls for the self-discipline of a budget, which most people do not want to place themselves under. But if you are serious about acquiring wealth, you will be serious about accumulating the funds that will enable you to turn opportunities into realities.

As soon as you have the money to do so, begin investing in tax-favoured ventures that make sense when the effects of inflation are considered. Expect inflation to continue robbing the ignorant and giving to the well-informed throughout this century; expect tax shelters to continue forever; expect America's population to continue to grow; expect the prices of everything to continue to fluctuate.

SELF-INSTRUCTIONS:

'I am wealthy. I'm wealthy because I think about the value that money has as a lifetime investment when I'm tempted to break out of my budget.'

'I live on____per cent of my income.'

73 The painfully obvious answer

I started off as a failure at college. Then I didn't make any money in my first attempts to break away from hourly paid jobs – in the beginning of my sales career I was a failure. Many of the people who knew me well years ago have asked, 'Tom, what happened to change your life so completely?'

The answer is almost painfully obvious to me now. But it certainly wasn't obvious back when I was struggling desperately –

not to make an outstanding income – simply to get by. If anyone was ever ready to succeed, it was me. That's the first step to success – you have to be utterly determined to succeed. But that's not the explanation of how I turned my life around.

Here's the painfully obvious answer: since I didn't know how to become a success, *that's what I had to learn*. Some people think that becoming a success means learning a job skill. The truth is that job skills play only a small part in anyone's success – a necessary part, certainly, but still only a small part. Success is ninety per cent self-discipline, attitude, and self-image – and only ten per cent job skill.

The greatest talent in the world is useless if the self-discipline to use it is lacking; the finest opportunity turns away when it meets a poor attitude; the best training leads only to failure if the self-image is bad.

If you're truly ready, the day will soon come when you turn your entire life around. You will open the right book, meet the right person, find the right need that you can fill, or see the right problem that you can make a fortune solving. You will become involved in the right experience and your life will change completely. If you're truly ready now, this book can start that process working for you today.

That's what happened to me. The start of my change came when I went to my first seminar. I had no money left. I was depressed. Luckily, a representative had come in some days previously and sold me on the seminar. The man teaching it was the late J. Douglas Edwards. Later he became my dearly loved friend.

When Mr Edwards walked out to begin that seminar, we were all in awe of this man because we had heard of his great success. He started off by saying, 'The one common characteristic that all successful people share is that they have their goals and their life outlined in writing.'

I felt guilty right away because I didn't have any written goals. It had never occurred to me to write any down – no one had ever suggested that to me, or told me how to do it.

J. Douglas Edwards taught me how and I started goal-setting. At the time, I was driving a beat-up Oldsmobile convertible with a rip the full length of the top. I had no money so I repaired the rip with silver tape – it looked like a racing stripe! The car was a junker and I was embarrassed to drive it, so for my first goal I wrote, 'I want a nice car.' After the seminar I got specific by touring the agencies and picking out the make, model, colour, and options I wanted.

When I mentioned this later to my friends, some of them said, 'Tom, don't drive an expensive car. People will think you're slick.' Average people don't want you to have anything better than they have. But I wrote down the expensive car as my first goal anyway. Ninety days later I got it. At first I thought it was just luck, but I said, 'I'll write another goal down, just in case.' In 1966, I wanted to be the top real estate salesperson in California as to the volume of transactions, so I wrote it down. I worked day and night to reach that goal. When I did reach it I thought, 'Maybe this is luck too.'

Gradually I began jotting down not only annual-income goals and status-symbol goals, but also personal-accomplishment goals of every kind. The day came when all of a sudden I could see exactly how goal-setting operates when you're truly ready. Then I started making a big thing of goals – getting them all down, adding details frequently, and making the hard decisions that are required to get rid of conflicts among them.

Focusing on goals to that extent caused me to start doing another vital thing; I began studying for a few hours every morning to learn the skills that would allow me to make all those goals come true.

And I always kept my goals with me. Very few people can reach into their wallet, pull out a card, and say, 'Here is my goal card. This is what I am well on the way to accomplishing.'

When you put your goals down in writing, you have set your direction. If you're ready for success, you will dwell on your goals; you will plan how you are going to reach them; you will learn what you have to learn; you will do everything that's required to make them come true.

So I'd like to share a few goal-setting tips with you now that are proven performers. I owe my achievements to them, as do many thousands of other successful people. Following these tips is the only way I know to ensure that your goals will impel you forward instead of blocking your drive to success. To push you forward, your goals must be great engines of purpose, excitement, and accomplishment, not wide swamps of confusion, disbelief, and futility.

We'll go over these goal-setting tips in the next section.

74   Goal-setting guidelines

Here are five conditions that must be worked into your goals. All are essential. Hitting four out of five is no good here – leave one condition out of a goal and that goal won't be reached. Put all five into a goal and you've got one that will become a reality in your life.

1. Your goals must be believable.
Let me repeat that: your goals *must* be believable. To whom? To only one person in the whole world – you. It doesn't matter who else believes in them – in fact, most of your goals should be too personal to reveal even to your spouse. But unless you believe that you can achieve them, you won't.

2. Your goals must be clearly defined.
If they're confused, if you're not sure *exactly* what your goals are, you don't have goals. Wishes maybe. Hopes perhaps. Goals, no. They must be specific, the more specific the better. You can say, 'Tom, I want to increase my net worth substantially,' but that's not a goal. That's only an idea, a starting place for creating a goal. What would make a goal? Deciding on the exact amount of net worth you want to have at a specific future date – one million dollars by December 31, 1999, for example. That's specific. That's clearly defined.

If you tell me, 'My short-term goal is to buy a new automobile. I really want one, Tom. I need to feel the pride that's associated with owning a new car' – all that is fine; it shows that you're gearing up to commit yourself to a goal. To make that goal happen, decide on all the specifics: what make, model, engine, colour – and when? Will you buy or lease? How much money will it take? Exactly how will you earn that money? You must be specific to be terrific.

3. Your goals must be ardently desired.

Not merely desired, *ardently* desired. When you want something so much that it eats on you, you'll get it. How do you cause yourself to ardently desire something? Read on.

4. Your goals must be vividly imagined.

If you can see yourself in possession of your goal, it's half yours. Form the habit of several times a day vividly imagining yourself having your goal; do that and it's in the palm of your hand.

Let me give you a very personal example of a believable, clearly defined, ardently desired and vividly imagined goal. Several years ago my sister Julie, whom I love dearly, weighed 279 pounds. When you're five-foot-two, that's a major problem.

When I realized she was ready to make a change, I spent an hour going over my goal-setting knowledge with her. Nineteen months later she had lost over 155 pounds. If you could see her happiness today at being able to wear a size 8, you'd not only know that this material works, you'd know that the joy of making it work is worth far more than the effort involved.

The key element that I suggested, the one she credits with making it possible for her to lose all that weight, was a very small thing. I asked her to go out and take a picture of the dress she wanted to wear. Then I told her to stare at that photo of a size 8 dress three times a day. While she was doing that, she was to imagine herself happily slipping that dress on and wearing it proudly.

Please believe me – when you weigh more than an eighth of a ton, when you hit the scales at nearly five pounds to the inch, wearing a size 8 looks as impossible as making a fortune looks when you're broke. She had to go through some pain to achieve her goal, didn't she? I'm proud of her for facing and beating that pain, more proud than words can express.

There's no change without pain. But Julie isn't feeling any of that pain anymore – that's all forgotten. She's changed her self-image enormously. She has the cutest little shape now and she's loving it, but the changes in her personality and life have gone far beyond that. Now she's an entirely new woman; she has a new sense of self-esteem, new interests, new opportunities, new confidence – and a whole range of new goals and successes. It all came from accepting the pain of change in order to attain a specific goal. Most people don't realize how quickly the pain of change is forgotten, and how long the benefits of achieving goals last and are enjoyed.

5. Your goals must be in writing.
This is such a vital requirement that I'm going to devote the next section to it.

SELF-INSTRUCTIONS:

'I take goal-setting seriously.'

'I have complete faith that I will achieve all my goals.'

'I ardently desire my goals because they're so exciting that they're never out of my mind for long.'

'I vividly imagine possessing all my goals three times a day.'

75 Writing your goals makes them glow

Let's review why it's so important to have *written* goals. I want to make this point strongly because I know that unless you put your goals in writing your chances of achieving them are quite small.

1. Written goals put verve in every day.
When you have achievable goals for every day written down, every day becomes an exciting contest with yourself. You get up in the morning with a plan for making that day contribute the most that it possibly can to getting what you want from life.

Dignify your goals by writing them down. Then you'll find that it's easy to jump out of bed and tell yourself, 'I'm excited about achieving this today.' Every morning you'll go charging out to make the most of your opportunities.

2. Written goals make extra effort easier.

When your goals are in writing, doing what you know needs doing is easier to stick with and harder to let slip. You have the important decisions made. Now converting your exciting goals into realities is a matter of following your plans.

3. Written goals generate enthusiasm.

The ability to set goals for yourself that are both achievable and exciting is a great skill. As with any great skill that you would acquire, this one demands persistent practice before it's yours. When it is, you'll discover that there's great power in the enthusiasm achievable and exciting goals generate when you have a commitment to them made in writing.

4. Written goals are great aids to getting organized.

If you have a problem with getting organized, you'll be delighted at how much written goals will help in putting you on a smooth track. Writing your goals lets you take charge of your life; it encourages you to make important decisions early instead of too late; it brings the conflicts in your plans into focus quickly so that you can eliminate them before problems develop; it highlights opportunities; it calls your attention to what needs to be done.

Have a set time each week for reviewing your progress, your goals, and your plans. The importance of having this weekly meeting with yourself can't be overemphasized. In no other way can you guarantee that your talent, technique, and time will be directed to best advantage at making your goals come true.

76 Goal-timing

Let's look at goals from the standpoint of timing. Not all goals should have a time limit. The purpose of giving yourself deadlines to achieve certain goals is to help you plan your life.

Don't put off setting lifetime goals. Sure, you'll change them. Changing your lifetime goals is a healthy process. As you learn more about the world, as you grow in emotional experience, as you achieve greater personal and career skills, your lifetime goals should change.

What allows you to learn the most and grow the fastest?

Setting a firm direction does. It's never too soon to set your lifetime goals, and never too late to change them. For most of us, long-term goals are the most difficult to decide on – we're really planning our entire life when we set serious long-term goals, aren't we?

Let me tell you what a long-term goal is. It's what you see yourself doing, being, and owning five or more years from now. To set long-term goals properly, you don't start with today, you go twenty years into the future. In my seminars when I say write down your twenty-year goals, the people sitting in front all gasp, 'Twenty years?' The trouble with the average person is that they don't plan even twenty days ahead, let alone twenty years.

A woman well along in years was sitting in front one morning when I said, 'Tonight, write down your twenty-year goals.' She looked up and winked. At the break she walked over and said, 'Tommy, I'm seventy-five years old. I just want to be here in twenty years!'

Guess what I made her do that night? Write it down. You may smile at that but a lot of longevity turns on the commitment to be here for a purpose. So you go twenty years, then back it up to ten years, then to five years. Plan your life. If you don't, who will?

Suppose that you had to sacrifice one of two things – your life or the building you're sitting in right now, which would it be? You'd save your life, of course. One life is more important than any material structure. Yet how is a building built? What had to be approved before one brick was laid, one piece of wood was bought, or one shovel of earth was dug. The plans. Blueprints. And what, in essence, are plans and blueprints? They are decisions about what's going to be. Many thousands of dollars are spent making those decisions and getting them down on the blueprints before anyone does any work at the new building's site. While the blueprints are being created, the money arrangements also are being worked out. Again, nobody does any work at the site until it's known how turning those plans into reality will be paid for.

Every life is worth more than any building, yet the average life has no blueprints for what it is to be, no plans for how it will be paid for. It's just a series of random happenings. Every day is another play-it-by-ear day.

A basic difference that separates the successful from the mediocre is that the successful plan their lives. Start with your entire life. Then back up to twenty years from now, then to ten, five, and three years from now. Your shortest long-term plan, and the one you'll work with most, is your one-year plan. How do you make a plan for your entire life work? One year at a time. How do you make a one-year plan work? One day at a time.

1. Begin by outlining your entire life.
What do you want to do with your entire life? Many thousands of things, of course. You can only list the general outline. Why bother? Because it allows you to make choices. It allows you to acquire the skills and knowledge you'll need, and to condition your mind and body to actually do what most like to do.

When do you want to retire from full-time moneymaking to a second career of some kind? What do you want your second career to be? Maybe you want to spend all your time in the mountains, fishing, or on a small boat. If you're under thirty, you might not want to give a second career or retirement much thought right now. Then don't. Come up with a quick general fix on your later decades and get on with detailing your nearer years. But before you reject the idea of making retirement plans now, please remember that some teenagers have set the goal of retiring with a substantial fortune before the age of thirty or forty, and then a few years later they achieved that goal. They wanted to pay the price and they did.

2. Drop back to your twenty-year goals.
Once you've set the general direction for your lifetime, start working on the details. The easiest place to begin is with the twenty-year span of time. Set a net worth goal; set goals in every area of your life; and then move back to who you want to be and what you want to be doing a decade from now.

3. Your ten-year goals.
What must you have accomplished in ten years to be on track for your twenty-year goals? Fortunately, you don't have to be halfway

there because the more wealth you have, the faster it compounds and grows.

4. Your five-year plan.
Now the reality of long-term goals will start coming into focus. A few minutes with a ten-dollar calculator will give you how much you must have in five years to be on schedule for your lifetime plan.

5. Your three-year plan.
Skip this one the first day you work on goals. In fact, it may be several weeks before you'll be ready to put together a three-year plan. Longer-term goals usually are brief; the three-year plan is one that many people use for their most important operating decisions.

6. Your next-twelve-months plan.
This is the budget, the working plan that you monitor at least once a week and roll forward once a month. In other words, when September of this year is over, you check your results against your 12-month forecast and then plan September of next year. Always keep your next twelve months planned.

Keep these plans simple. Limit them to essentials. Base them on numbers: money earned, people seen, this kind of thing. Your 12-month plan is an outline for action, not an essay on intention.

7. Your next month's plan.
Give this one some serious thought as you work your way through the current month. Set a time each month – the fifteenth is a good day – to complete your plan for next month. Keep this with you so that you can make appointments and other decisions quickly and finally.

8. Your next week's plan.
For most people this is the key time planning tool.

9. Your tomorrow's plan.
This is your *six most important things to do tomorrow* list that was discussed in section 56.

* * *

Don't let the idea of planning your life overwhelm you. Put it in writing so that you can add to it as you go along. Use a looseleaf three-ring binder, a school notebook, for your lifeplan. Once you've made your first fast pass through all these plans in the order given above, work back from next year's plan to your twenty-year plan.

On your second pass, you'll find that many adjustments are required. Most people make several passes before their plans come together and take on the aspect of reality. When they do that, you're really blasting for success.

Add excitement to your planning by including all the fun things you want. Make planning a pleasure, not a duty. If your plans are nothing but grim sets of numbers, you'll soon lose interest in them. Your lifeplan should be a thriller in your own terms, not a bore.

Look at each thing you want and decide whether getting it is a long-term or a short-term goal. Ninety days is the limit for short-term goals. If you have short-term goals that'll take longer than three months to reach, you'll lose interest in them. Break up any goal that requires more time into pieces, each one of which you can achieve within ninety days.

What do you want for yourself? You're the only one who knows what you really want. Make sure that your plans are loaded with things that you selfishly want for yourself.

Goal-setting should be great fun. Make sure you keep it that way. Then your goal-achieving will be even more fun – and more certain.

77 All the goals you need

How do you go about deciding what goals to set? Where do you begin? Begin where you can gain the most lift for your life. Let's examine the general areas:

1. Money.
Since money impacts on almost everything we do or hope to do, it's the first area that most of us need to set goals in. Money goals will be discussed in the next section, so we won't go into them here.

2. Health.

Setting goals to become and stay healthier might strike you as strange – unless you've had some serious health problems. Most of us tend to ignore our health most of the time until we create a problem. To a great degree your health is as good as you truly want it to be – good health is no accident. It springs from a healthy mental attitude towards life and sensible habits.

3. Family.

You can help set goals for your family as a group, but you can't set goals for each of your family members – they have to set their own goals.

Include your family in setting goals that your spouse, children, and other family memebers will all work as a team on. Some of these goals might be acquiring a swimming pool, taking a vacation, starting a business. Many years ago at a goal-setting family meeting, I asked Timmy, 'What do you really want?' My son said, 'Dad, I'd love a new ten-speed.'

I said, 'Good. If Dad gets ten listings next month, you get it.' He would not let me come home! He became a part of my productivity. 'Dad, how're you doing? You canvassing? Get out of here. Did you send them thank-you notes? Let's get to work.'

4. Personal accomplishments.

What do you see yourself doing in twenty years? Start visualizing what you want to be in the future. Do you want to be a lawyer, doctor, the leader of a company? Perhaps you want to distinguish yourself in public service. Start visualizing it. See it in your future. Write it down and start developing the detailed plans that'll make it possible. Maybe you want to learn French, hot-air ballooning, or guitar. Along with your career goals, make sure that you include some fun things too. River-rafting, skiing, seeing the world – write it down as a goal so you'll be able to do it all.

5. Status symbols.

What goodies have you've always wanted? After a seminar recently, I sat with a man who came through my training eight years ago and today is very successful at putting things like companies and properties together. He said, 'Tom, I want to drive a Rolls-Royce someday.'

'Someday?'

'Well, within – ' He thought a minute. 'Actually, I want it this year.'

'It's important to you?'

'Very.'

'Then write it down.'

Today he's happily driving his Rolls-Royce. You might say, 'I wouldn't want one.' Then that's not important to you. What is important is to have the status symbols that say the right things to you and about you – the possessions, achievements, and marks of distinction that tell the world, 'I've accomplished something with my life.'

Your status symbols may not be materialistic. They certainly don't have to be. Some people want to give their children a great start in life; this is what my parents wanted. Others want to discover something, create something, hold an office, be a power in the community or the nation. The essential thing is to want the status symbols that please you and fit your career goals.

6. Set up accomplishment rewards for yourself.

You only get the reward if you reach a goal that involves doing something specific and important – but no goal, no goodie. It's easy to say, 'I'm going to get that new car in three months,' without tying that reward to any financial achievement. Then when you go down to pick it up all you do is put yourself in debt.

Set up accomplishment goals backed by rewards. 'I'm going to achieve such and such. When I've done that, I'm going to reward myself with my dream item.'

78   The two money approaches to goals

Fame is fleeting – but money that's invested well can linger in your family for generations. Everybody I know who has achieved a noteworthy degree of financial status understands the two basic ways of looking at money: the income statement and the net worth statement. Up-and-comers have a complete grasp of both these financial tools and they keep track of their own positions with them. For details, they rely on the statements that their accountants produce. For decision-making and goal-setting, the up-and-comers can always recall and add up the basic figures that apply to their current situation.

In his heyday Howard Hughes could pencil out an accurate net worth statement for himself from memory. Sometimes he forgot two or three items on his first run through – maybe a $30 million dollar subsidiary here and a $25 million property there – but he'd pick them up when he doublechecked his figures. Some of his largest decisions were made off the quick calculations he scribbled on a scrap of paper and then tore up as soon as he'd made up his mind. Hughes understood taxes and accounting – as does everyone who makes it and then manages to keep the money.

Use these two basic statements to set your money goals and to keep track of your progress at teaching them. The income statement tells you what you're making; the net worth statement tells you how much of it you're keeping.

If you're not at home with these two basic accounting views of your money position, take a bookkeeping or accounting class at your local night school. Then start making out monthly income statements for your own personal operation. Every ninety days, make out a net worth statement. If you're an employee now, don't wait until you're self-employed because, in reality, you are self-employed now. Everything that you make above what you spend is your profit. That's your only true income.

Some of us don't realize that we're self-employed even though we're punching in five days a week. Let's look at an executive who makes a $300,000 salary and spends $299,999 of it. Compare him to his number two man. Number two makes $75,000 a year and lives on $50,000. Although the executive is paid four times as much as number two is, he isn't making a profit on his year's work. When the year has passed, he has nothing to show for his efforts. Number two, on the other hand, is operating at an impressive 33⅓ per cent profit on his work. With the $25,000 he's accumulated from one year's labour, he'll add substantially to his investments; already he's in a position to take advantage of opportunities that his boss would have to pass up.

A lack of self-discipline nails the executive to his job, but his assistant is free to move in any direction that offers him a better return for his time and talent.

Now let's take a closer look at how the income and net worth statements fit into the goal-setting activity that's going to make you rich.

1. Income.

The income statement shows what you earned, spent, and brought down to the bottom line. Don't look for higher earnings, look for higher net, net, net profits. Net after all costs of doing business, net after all personal expenditures, net after taxes – the dollars that are left are the only ones available to make your longer-term goals real. Plan your future by preparing an income statement in advance that lists all your expenses and income. Then, as the year goes by, you can easily check how you're doing. If your net profit is below your forecast, take action to raise your earnings or cut your expenses.

2. Net worth.

All of us have seen a lot of changes in our world and in our society. I really believe we all have to start saying to ourselves, 'No one is going to take care of me but me.' For years we've been sold on the concept that from the day we start working, we're working for retirement.

Retirement is another word for an early death. It's true for many people. The records prove that when people become inactive in retirement, their lives are shortened drastically. If it wasn't so sad, it would be funny to think about how many young people are taught to work to retire.

You don't work to retire, you work to be fulfilled. People stay on jobs they hate because of that rosy dream of the day they'll get the gold watch and the pension and retire to do whatever they please. The problem is that their inflation-ravaged pensions hardly cover the barest necessities of life, and leave nothing to pay for the activities that make free time really enjoyable.

It's our obligation to be ready when the times comes to enjoy our golden years. That's why you write down your net worth goals. What do you want for a net worth then? A million dollars? In twenty years it won't be that much, so why not? You want to be able to look at your spouse and say, 'We did it, kid. Let's take the cruise and have some fun.'

Let's talk about the meaning of *want* as it applies here. When it comes to goals, the only things you want are those you're willing to pay the price for. There may be a lot of other things that you wish and hope for; but since you're not willing to pay the price for them, you're not going to get them. So those things have no place at all in your goal setting. What you want you must pay the price for. What net worth are you willing to pay the price for?

Sit down with your spouse and discuss this entire concept. If you've been working up the enthusiasm to sacrifice for goals and your spouse hasn't been in on this new line of thinking, you can be sure that he or she won't be with you at first. Give your partner time to learn about, adjust to, and contribute to your new interest in goal-setting and success. Don't barge in and say, 'All right, we're going to start living on forty-two per cent of our income and have a million bucks in six years – then we'll start enjoying ourselves. But until then, it's going to be tight city.' You can give somebody a terrific shock. This approach is guaranteed to sink your goals in bitter argument instead of launching them on a flood of enthusiasm.

Begin by pencilling out a net worth statement that balances what you own today with your debts and net worth. Put a fair market value on everything you own and add up all those selling prices. The total will be your total assets, not your net worth – don't ever let yourself think otherwise.

Next, list how much you owe. Include every debt that you have; add all your debts up, and write down the total. Now subtract what you owe from what you own. The figure that's left, your net worth, is the number that counts.

For planning and goal setting, you want to work up two net worth statements. The first is today's reality, that is, it shows what you own, owe, and are worth today. Next, make up your twenty-year net worth goal statement. In other words, start developing a statement of exactly how your net worth will be realized. Begin with a list of how much cash, stocks and bonds, notes and deeds receivable, real estate, and other property you want to have. List what you want to own, and what you're willing to owe against those assets then (if anything), and what you want to be worth when what you owe is subtracted from what you want to own in twenty years.

Write those three figures down on a card that you keep with you. Refer to them frequently.

I would be so flattered to have you work out with your spouse the net worth figure, the cash-out-in-thirty-days bottom-line figure, that you want to have in twenty years. Then start working back to today. The work-back is the whole purpose of this procedure because this leads to action that you'll take in the coming months and years to make your goals come true.

SELF-INSTRUCTIONS:

'I understand that I really am self-employed even though I have a job at _____.'

'I never forget that accumulating capital for investment opportunities is the key that opens the door to success.'

'I have plenty of self-discipline, so I always meet my goal of saving ____ per cent of my income for investment.' (Ten per cent is the lowest savings figure that makes any sense at all, and if you're aiming high, you must set your saving goal much higher.)

'I am ready for the next step in my climb upward.'

79   Cut your chains to yesterday

Some people would rather live in the time they know, the past. They'd rather think about what they had, or what they could have had if things had gone the way they should. By concentrating their attention on the unchangeable past, they limit their future. When you're living in the past, your real self ceases to exist because your real self is what you are at this moment, not what you were at any time in the near or distant past.

A great philosopher once said, 'You can never stand in the same river.' Life, changes, and time are flowing all around us at this instant in eternity.

Many people hang mental handicaps on themselves by reliving their previous difficulties over and over. If you inflict your past wounds on the present, you'll make your future bleed.

Cut your chains to the past. Begin by putting a solid block on living up to the image that other people have of you. When people start telling you how you are, it's a dead giveaway that they're trying to control you. Spouses often work this field. Next to financial pressure, the biggest marriage problems that people are having in our society stem from one spouse trying to stifle the growth of the other. You can't do that today. I love the little saying, 'Set whatever you have free, and if it comes back to you it's yours. If it doesn't, it never was.'

Know when you're playing a role or wearing a mask. We all have to play roles; we all have to wear masks – this is part of life. Many people say, 'I'm just myself with everybody.' You can do that but you're not going to be very popular. Some of these same people say, 'I don't like phonies.'

You don't have to be a phony to accept the fact that we have to communicate with our fellow human beings effectively if we're going to be successful. I'd like to tell a few people – a very few – who are at my seminars where to go, but I don't. There's more good than bad in everybody. To achieve in this life you must always look for the good because achievements are only built of good things.

Too many of us dwell on what people don't have. Think about this in all your personal relationships: your marriage, your family, your close friends. Whenever the barriers are broken down and you are close to another person, have you ever noticed how prone we are to gradually swing over and concentrate on the negatives? We start to analyze the lackings, the shortcomings. Don't do that. Focus on the good points that other people have – especially the good points that all those who are close to you have.

Think about why you're tempted to feel the need to concentrate on the negative things about someone who is important to you. You're tempted because you're dependent on that person for friendship, acceptance, prestige, for any of a large number of things. This is good – the alternative is to be a hermit or an outcast of some kind   but being dependent on other people does give them the power to withhold important things from you. That power, even though it might never be used, can make you anxious. And since you have identified yourself with those people or that person, your ego is involved in what they do and how well they do it. Their failures become your failures and are often more frustrating than your own because you can do so little to prevent them.

If you're feeling any of these things keenly, they are blocking your drive for success. Put this in perspective by determining to be yourself. Say to yourself, 'I'm going to be better so that other people will be closer and care more about me.'

Do this by embarking on a new activity as soon as you master what you're doing now. Don't get caught in a rut. Ruts are easier to begin with, they get depressing fast, and nothing is harder than being depressed.

Most people cut their deepest ruts at work. If you're in business for yourself as a salesperson or as an owner, you are free of the walls that make it harder for most people to steer out of ruts. So many people wake up about the same time every day. They get into the same car every day. They drive to the same job every day. They live for lunch every workday morning; they live for the time clock's final gong every afternoon. When you're in sales or some other form of self-employment, you can honestly say that you're in charge of your day. This means that you determine whether any given day will be productive or not.

But there are many little ruts the self-employed can get into – the early stop for a long cup of coffee, the newspaper that has to be read all the way through in the morning, the loose routing that lets you run at half speed all day. If we're not constantly alert for new ways to make ourselves more efficient, if we're not working to meet our own goals, we can find plausible reasons to slide into these little ruts that quickly add up to lost months of time.

Learn to distinguish between efficient organization and time-wasting rut-running. What is the difference between the loser's ruts and the winner's routine? The difference is in why they are followed. The loser loves his ruts because they let him avoid reality and slip into temporary comfort; the winner loves his efficient habits because they give him more time and energy for facing reality and taking on new challenges.

How does holding on to the past hurt your life? If you constantly think of past benefits, previous jobs, and former relationships, you create a feeling of insecurity. If you dwell on what you used to have, it'll always seem better than you thought it was when you had it. Time heals all wounds, and then helps you think that what you hated in the past wasn't all that bad. It's good to forget past pain. But you can do that without replacing the reality of yesterday with thoughts of what never was. Dreaming of a false past keeps an enormous number of people from moving effectively in the present. Remember the thorns along with the roses when the past comes to mind. If you dwell on the security of a former relationship, what you're really saying is, 'I'm not secure today, but I was secure in the past.' You weren't, of course.

You're as secure today as your ability to cope with insecurity. No one will ever be more secure than that.

SELF-INSTRUCTIONS:

'I live in the present.'

'I always look for the good in the people close to me.'

'Without being careless of my own interests, I look for the good in everyone.'

'I'm glad that I'm dependent on my family for love and a sense of belonging.'

'I use habit to speed routine, not to block out reality.'

'I have many fond memories, but I also remember that the past had its share of daily frustrations and problems too.'

80 The name of the game of success

What is the one thing that you must have to succeed? It's a little thing called self-discipline – something that's little only in the sense that it's yours any time you choose to take it. In its effect on your life, having self-discipline makes a tremendous difference – a difference too great to measure. It's not something you're given, not something you inherit; self-discipline is something that you acquire by yourself. You get it from the inner person, from the voice that talks to you all the time.

When you have self-discipline from that inner source, you can transmit some of it to others. Self-discipline is the foundation of self-improvement. It channels your resources of time, energy, and money into the habit of learning and growing towards something new and better each and every day. I believe in surrounding myself with happy and successful people; I believe that happiness and self-discipline are found together, and that together they are the fountain of greatness.

People who achieve success share at least this one thing called self-discipline. Regardless of the endeavour – whether they are professional people, students in school, business owners, corporate executives, or whatever – the one characteristic that is common to all succeeders is self-discipline.

I'm sure you'll agree that the average person on this continent today has a problem with self-discipline. We have a very entertainment-conscious, fun-orientated, and excitement-loving population. In 1925, President Calvin Coolidge said, 'The business of America is business.' If he were alive today, could he say that again with a straight face? In less than sixty years we've turned into a don't-work-too-hard society. Could that explain some paradoxes? With the greatest economic base that any population in history ever had, our government is staggering under its debt load, taxes are so high that new enterprise is discouraged, and millions of able-bodied people are on welfare. At the same time, millions of illegal immigrants are swarming into this country to take jobs that Americans won't accept. Can it be that our don't-work-too-hard attitude explains why we're importing instead of manufacturing everything from Automobiles to Zippers?

It's easy to rise above the performance level of the masses because the masses today do not want to be disciplined. But they do want much, much more from life. What they don't realize is that those two wants are incompatible. Achieving success when we have dedication, commitment, and self-discipline is almost a certainty in North America today; when we don't have these qualities, it's almost impossible.

Some of us weren't disciplined when we were young. Without a background of discipline, it's harder to become self-disciplined. But it's only a little harder – don't lay any lack of drive and discipline that you may have at your parents' door. It may have been their responsibility before your teens, but when you moved into your second dozen years on this earth the responsibility became yours. No matter how they raised you, it's your life now – it's your success that you're disciplining yourself for, not theirs.

To develop self-discipline is to take possession of your mind with such strength that your emotions and appetites are brought under control. That's really what you do to achieve self-discipline – you literally take possession. You tell yourself, 'I control my body; I control my mind; I control my actions; I control events in my territory.' It's called willpower. It's called self-discipline. It's called self-control. It's doing what you know you should do. It's avoiding what you know you should not do.

When you have that extra force of willpower, you grow away from the people who are allowing their lives to drift. Your self-discipline begins with your positive thoughts, their indiscipline begins with their negative thoughts. Those who fail to control their thoughts are unable to control their deeds. The things that happen to you are the result of the actions you take. The actions you take are the result of the feelings that you have. The feelings you have are the result of the thoughts you allow in your mind. So, to control what happens to you, begin by saying, 'I control my thoughts.' Through the power of self-discipline, balance the emotions of the heart with the reasonings of the mind.

When you achieve that combination, you have created a very powerful human being. The person who controls himself or herself through self-discipline can never be controlled by others.

SELF-INSTRUCTIONS:

'I control my thoughts.'
'I don't let negative ideas enter my mind.'
'I control my mind, my body, and my actions.'
'I control events in ＿＿＿＿＿＿＿＿＿＿＿＿.'

81 Another look at the big SD

Self-Discipline really encompasses nearly everything in life. Do you remember in school when you were given thirty days to write a term paper? Did you start it that first night?

Most of us didn't. Instead, we thought about it every night, 'Got to get moving on that ratty project. But I've got almost a whole month left – it can wait.' As time goes by, worry about getting a failing grade looms larger in our minds. At first the pain of starting the term paper is greater than our concern about the failing grade, so after a week we still haven't started. Two weeks go by. What are we doing every night before we go to sleep? Worrying about that F. 'I better start. Tomorrow I'll get moving on it.'

A week before the term paper is due, the F is getting larger – but it's still not quite large enough to offset the pain of working at preventing it. All of a sudden there are only three days left before it's due, and at last the F looms larger than the pain of working on the term paper. So we start.

As you lay it out you begin feeling some enthusiasm. 'This isn't bad. I may get an A if I do this and do that.' When you walk in with your paper you're happy, but you wasted twenty-seven days worrying about starting. In other words, you operated at a deficit emotionally for twenty-seven days when you could have been in the profit column all the time. Move into the emotional profit column right now; starting today, get your priority tasks and actions done promptly. Plan your actions, then act on your plans. Apply this determination to every area of your life and it will make an enormous difference in your income and growth rate in business and your satisfaction and growth rate personally.

The portrait of a man who was being called the Whiz Kid of

Wall Street appeared on the cover of a national magazine a few years ago. He was one of the first to put a conglomerate together, and some of the federal laws affecting business in the early seventies came about because of the trends that his creativity set off. At the time he was forty-two; he was running one of the largest industrial combines in the country, the conglomerate he had built himself. So the magazine had assigned a journalist and a team of researchers to do an in-depth report on this entrepreneur.

One of the researchers went to the small city the dynamic executive had left fifteen years earlier. A few items turned up there about an alcoholic with the same name who had been sleeping on park benches at that time. The researcher passed this information along, and as the journalist was concluding his interview with the Wall Street powerhouse in his plush office, the journalist laughed and said, 'Believe it or not, a man with your exact name was sleeping on park benches and getting rousted by the police when you lived in your hometown. I guess the poor guy was a real wino. Isn't that something?'

The president looked up and smiled. 'That was me.'

'This can't be. You're kidding.'

The president of the conglomerate leaned back in his leather chair and shook his head. 'I'm not kidding. The wino sleeping off drunks on park benches was me.'

The journalist stared at him for a moment and saw that he was telling the truth. He also realized that now he had a whole new story. When his apologies were waved aside, he said, 'What made you change?'

Listen to what he said because so many people fit this mould: 'When I was sleeping under newspapers in the park fifteen years ago, I knew that someday I would do what I'm doing now. I was just waiting until I was ready to start.'

Do you know how many people are like that? 'Well, next year's my year. I'm going to get to work then. You just wait and see – right after the first of the year I'm gonna start shaping up.' But of course the time to get going never quite comes for most people.

Don't wait. Time is flying by so fast. So very fast. Start today to achieve the greatness you know is in you.

SELF-INSTRUCTIONS:

'I know that success depends on how I use my time, so I always use it exceedingly well.'

'I'm self-disciplined. When I make commitments to myself or to others, I keep them.'

'I'm proud of my record, proud of my willingness to do what I know must be done, proud of the fact that I'm a shaker, breaker, and doer.'

82   How many can you handle?

What's the best number of self-instructions to work with at one time? How many can you benefit from simultaneously? The more the better, but there's a clear-cut limit. That limit is the number of them that you will repeat two or three times a day, taking long enough with each one to bring its emotions into sharp focus so that you can feel their power.

Reviewing your entire batch of active self-instructions shouldn't involve more than about a minute for each of your three sessions a day. One minute gives you four seconds to feel fifteen different self-instructions. Making a habit of this system takes three weeks. After you have this habit, you'll discover that you can easily get into the emotions of a self-instruction in four seconds. Repetition is what counts, the several-times-a-day repetition of keenly felt emotions will have a great cumulative impact on your actions.

For most people, fifteen is about the right number of self-instructions to start reviewing. Keep your review sessions short and snappy so you won't have any difficulty finding time for them. You can always spare one minute three times a day. After you've gained skill at doing this, you may want to work with more than fifteen self-instructions at a time.

Take a stack of 3 x 5 cards and write out every self-instruction you think could help you, one on each card. Snap a rubber band around fifteen of them and call that bunch your active instructions.

Those fifteen cards are your first textbook for intensifying your faith in yourself. Put the rest of the cards in your reserve pack.

Rotate a card from your active pack to your reserve pack whenever you feel that you've made a large improvement in the area covered by that card. You'll be surprised at how quickly this will occur with many of the self-instructions. When you have some clear-cut successes, will you be convinced that self-instructions are your ticket to every goal you really want? If so, intensify your use of this system.

The successes will certainly happen if you follow the system faithfully. Start off with at least ten self-instructions about small things – little habits you want to make or break – so you will get quick proof that self-instructions work.

To achieve the most powerful results with this system in the shortest time, set a half hour aside every week for a concentrated session with your self-instructions. Use this time to add new ones, to review both your reserve and active cards, and to think up more emotional ways of working your most important self-instructions. This half hour will give you time to get into your instructions deeply enough to feel the emotions behind each one intensely. This is a skill that takes practice to develop. If you'll turn this system on full blast, you'll discover that it's the most rewarding skill you'll ever learn from a book.

ONE FINAL SET OF SELF-INSTRUCTIONS:

'I review my self-instructions every morning and night and at least once more during the day. I take a few seconds with each self-instruction to feel its emotions intensely.'

'When I feel my self-instructions, I look out of my eyes as the person I'm becoming. I look at the world not as the person I am, but as who I want to be. I feel myself doing the things I want to do, and for those vital instants I am who I want to be.'

'Every week I spend half an hour adding new self-instructions, revising old ones and intensifying my emotional involvement with them.'

'I do all this because I am the effective, hard-driving, and highly successful kind of person who responds well to positive self-instruction.'

Mr Hopkins conducts sales training seminars and motivational programmes internationally. When time is available, he also accepts a limited number of personal speaking engagements.

A complete sales training programme entitled 'How to Master the Art of Selling Anything' is also available for both individual and company use on audio cassettes and on video tape.

For information on Tom Hopkins sales training seminars, video tape training programmes, and personal-use audio cassette albums, call or write:

Tom Hopkins
P.O. Box 1969
Scottsdale, Arizona 85252
(602) 949–0786

Recommended reading list

Addington, Jack E. *All About Goals and How to Achieve Them*. Marina Del Rey, Ca.: De Vorss Co., 1977.

Anderson, Uell. S. *The Magic in Your Mind*. North Hollywood, Ca.: Wilshire Book Co., 1966.

——. Three Magic Words. North Hollywood, Ca.: Wilshire Book Co., 1966.

Bristol, Claude M. *The Magic of Believing*. New York: Cornerstone Library, 1967.

Campbell, David. *If You Don't Know Where You are Going You Will Probably End Up Somewhere Else*. Allen, Texas: Argus Communications, 1974.

Carnegie, Dale. *How to Win Friends and Influence People*. New York: Simon & Schuster, 1936. New York: Pocket Books, 1981.

——. *How to Stop Worrying and Start Living*. New York: Simon & Schuster, 1948. New York: Pocket Books, 1977.

Curtis, Donald. *Your Thoughts Can Change Your Life*. North Hollywood, Ca.: Wilshire Book Co., 1969.

Douglas, Mack R. *How to Make a Habit of Succeeding*. Grand Rapids, Mich.: Zondervan Publishing House, 1974.

Dyer, Wayne. *Your Erroneous Zones*. Philadelphia: Thomas. Y. Crowell Co., 1976. New York: Avon, 1981.

———. *Pulling Your Own Strings*. New York: Avon, 1981.

Engstrom, Ted and Alec MacKenzie. *Managing Your Time*. Grand Rapids, Mich.: Zondervan, 1968.

Friedman, Meyer and Ray H. Rosenman. *Type A Behavior and Your Heart*. New York: Knopf, 1974.

Glasser, William. *Reality Therapy*. New York: Harper & Row, 1965.

Greenberg, Samuel. *Neurosis Is a Painful Style of Living*. New York: New American Library, 1978.

Greenburg, Dan. *How to Make Yourself Miserable*. New York: Random House, 1976.

Greenwald, Jerry. *Be the Person You were Meant to Be*. New York: Dell, 1979.

Hayden, Naura. *Everything You've Always Wanted to Know About Energy . . . But Were Too Weak to Ask*. New York: Hawthorne Books, 1976.

Harris, Sidney J. *The Authentic Person: Dealing With Dilemma*. Allen, Texas: Argus Communications, 1972.

Hill, Napoleon. *Think and Grow Rich*. New York: Fawcett, 1979.

Hopkins, Tom. *How to Master the Art of Selling*. Scottsdale, Ariz.: Champion Press, 1980. New York: Warner Books, 1982.

James, Muriel and Dorothy Jongeward. *Born to Win*. New York: New American Library, 1978.

Jourard, Sidney M. *The Transparent Self: Self-Disclosure & Well-Being*. New York: Van Nostrand Reinhold, 1971.

Kennedy, Eugene. *If You Really Knew Me, Would You Still Like Me?* Allen, Texas: Argus Communications, 1975.

LaHaye, Tim. *How to Win Over Depression.* Grand Rapids, Mich.: Zondervan, 1974.

Lakein, Alan. *How to Get Control of Your Time and Life.* New York: Peter H. Wyden Inc., 1973. New York: Signet, 1974.

Lindberg, Anne Morrow. *Gift From the Sea.* New York: Random House, 1953.

Maltz, Maxwell, *Psycho-Cybernetics and Self-Fulfillment.* New York: North Hollywood, Ca.: Wilshire Book Co., 1963.

——. *Thoughts to Live By.* New York: Pocket Books, 1981.

——. *Live and Be Free Through Psycho-Cybernetics.* New York: Warner Books, 1978.

Missildine, Hugh W. *Your Inner Child of the Past.* New York: Simon & Schuster, 1974.

Murphy, Joseph. *The Power of Your Subconscious Mind.* Englewood Cliffs, NJ: Prentice-Hall, 1963.

Olson, Ken. *Can You Wait 'til Friday: Psychology of Hope.* Phoenix, Ariz.: O'Sullivan, Woodside & Co., 1975.

Osborne, Cecil. *The Art of Understanding Yourself.* Grand Rapids, Mich.: Zondervan, 1968.

Paulus, Trina. *Hope for the Flowers.* New York: Paulist Press, 1972.

Peale, Norman Vincent. *The Power of Positive Thinking.* Englewood Cliffs, NJ: Prentice-Hall, 1954. New York: Fawcett, 1978.

——. *The Positive Principle Today*. Englewood Cliffs, NJ: Prentice-Hall, 1976. New York: Fawcett, 1981.

Powell, John. *Why Am I Afraid to Tell You Who I Am?* Allen, Texas: Argus Communications, 1969.

Schindler, John A. *How to Live Three Hundred Sixty-Five Days a Year*. New York: Fawcett, 1978.

Schuller, Robert. *Move Ahead With Possibility Thinking*. New York: Doubleday, 1967. New York: Jove, 1973.

Stone, W. Clement and Napoleon Hill. *Success Through a Positive Mental Attitude*. Englewood Cliffs, NJ: Prentice-Hall, 1960.

Wagner, Maurice. *The Sensation of Being Somebody*. Grand Rapids, Mich.: Zondervan, 1975.

Wilson, Tom. *Never Get Too Personally Involved with Your Own Life*. Mission, Kansas: Andrews & McMeel, 1975.

——. *Ziggys of the World Unite*. New York: New American Library, 1977.

Serious Creativity
Using the Power of Lateral Thinking
to Create New Ideas

Edward de Bono

The lack of fresh, constructive thinking is the vital missing ingredient in the way many businesses and people tackle the problem of the 1990s. With *Serious Creativity*, world-renowned Edward de Bono brings right up to date his landmark concept of lateral thinking, drawing on twenty-five years of practical experience on the deliberate use of creativity.

Creativity is becoming increasingly important for all businesses as competition intensifies, because it is the best and cheapest way to get added value out of existing resources and assets. New concepts are essential for the 'Sur/Petition' that is coming to replace traditional competition. Edward de Bono's *Serious Creativity* has undoubtedly become *the* standard textbook of creativity around the world, demonstrating that his techniques of lateral thinking do work for individuals *and* corporations.

With this step-by-step approach to creativity on demand, creative thinking at last becomes a usable skill instead of a matter of talent, temperament – or just luck.

ISBN 0 00 637958 3

Managing Yourself

Mike Pedler and Tom Boydell

How well do you manage yourself?
Are you in control of your ideas, feelings and actions?
Does your life have purpose and direction?
Have you enough personal energy?

Anyone who wants to improve the way they manage others must first learn to manage themselves. Starting from the inside out, managers need to become more aware of what they are doing in the areas of:

- health – physical, mental and emotional
- skills – social and technical
- action – how you get things done
- identity – valuing and being yourself

This practical guide for the 'thinking manager' contains case studies and useful activities to undertake which are designed to help you increase your effectiveness in managing yourself and your life and in improving your performance both at work and elsewhere.

Published in cooperation with The Association for Management Education and Development.

ISBN 0 00 636892 1

☐ MAKING IT HAPPEN: REFLECTIONS ON LEADERSHIP
John Harvey-Jones   0-00-638341-6   £6.99
☐ MADE IN JAPAN: AKIO MORITA AND SONY Akio Morita   0-00-638342-4   £6.99
☐ ODYSSEY: PEPSI TO APPLE
John Sculley with John A. Byrne   0-00-638343-2   £6.99

These books are available from your local bookseller or can be ordered direct from the publishers.
To order direct just tick the titles you want and fill in the form below:

Name:

Address:

Postcode:

Send to: HarperCollins Mail Order, Dept 8, HarperCollins*Publishers*, Westerhill Road, Bishopbriggs, Glasgow G64 2QT.
Please enclose a cheque or postal order or your authority to debit your Visa/Access account –

Credit card no:

Expiry date:

Signature:

– to the value of the cover price plus:
UK & BFPO: Add £1.00 for the first and 25p for each additional book ordered.

Overseas orders including Eire, please add £2.95 service charge.

Books will be sent by surface mail but quotes for airmail despatches will be given on request.

24 HOUR TELEPHONE ORDERING SERVICE FOR
ACCESS/VISA CARDHOLDERS –
TEL: GLASGOW 041-772 2281 or LONDON 081-307 4052